AIMING FOR AN A

IN

PS

A-LEVEL

PSYCHOLOGY

Jean-Marc Lawton

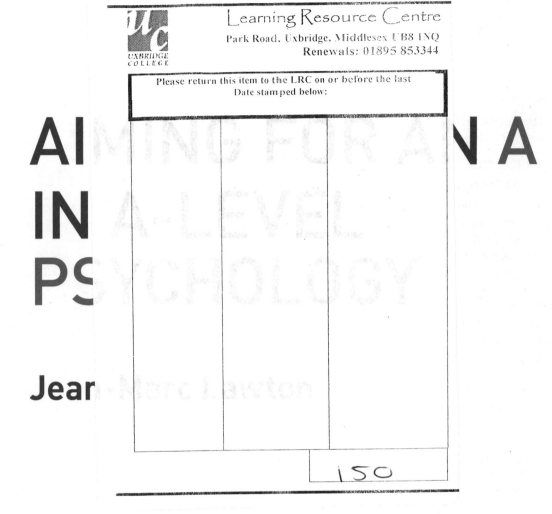

HODDER
EDUCATION
AN HACHETTE UK COMPANY

The Publishers would like to thank the following for permission to reproduce copyright material:

pp.12–13 mathematical skills table, © Crown Copyright 2014, licensed under the Open Government Licence v3.0.

Acknowledgements

With thanks to the CDARE team at the Sheffield Institute of Education for their assistance in developing and reviewing this title.

Every effort has been made to trace all copyright holders, but if any have been inadvertently overlooked, the Publishers will be pleased to make the necessary arrangements at the first opportunity.

Although every effort has been made to ensure that website addresses are correct at time of going to press, Hodder Education cannot be held responsible for the content of any website mentioned in this book. It is sometimes possible to find a relocated web page by typing in the address of the home page for a website in the URL window of your browser.

Hachette UK's policy is to use papers that are natural, renewable and recyclable products and made from wood grown in sustainable forests. The logging and manufacturing processes are expected to conform to the environmental regulations of the country of origin.

Orders: please contact Bookpoint Ltd, 130 Park Drive, Milton Park, Abingdon, Oxon OX14 4SE. Telephone: (44) 01235 827720. Fax: (44) 01235 400401. Email education@bookpoint.co.uk Lines are open from 9 a.m. to 5 p.m., Monday to Saturday, with a 24-hour message answering service. You can also order through our website: www.hoddereducation.co.uk

ISBN: 978 1 5104 2423 4

© Jean-Marc Lawton 2018

First published in 2018 by
Hodder Education,
An Hachette UK Company
Carmelite House
50 Victoria Embankment
London EC4Y 0DZ

www.hoddereducation.co.uk

Impression number   10 9 8 7 6 5 4 3 2 1

Year   2022 2021 2020 2019 2018

Typeset in Integra Software Services Pvt. Ltd., Pondicherry, India

Printed in Spain

A catalogue record for this title is available from the British Library.

Getting the most from this book

Aiming for an A is designed to help you master the skills you need to achieve the highest grades. The following features will help you get the most from this book.

Learning outcomes

> **A summary of the skills that will be covered in the chapter.**

Exam tip

Practical advice about how to apply your skills to the exam.

Activity

An opportunity to test your skills with practical activities.

! Common pitfall

Problem areas where candidates often miss out on marks.

The difference between...

Explanations of key differences that make A-grade students stand out.

Annotated example

Exemplar answers with commentary showing how to achieve top grades.

Worked example

Step-by-step examples to help you construct effective answers to exam questions and carry out mini-practicals.

Take it further

Suggestions for further reading or activities that will stretch your thinking.

You should know

> **A summary of key points to take away from the chapter.**

Contents

About this book

The A-grade student

A-level psychology will generally be a new subject for most students. You don't need a GCSE in psychology to study it at A-level, but you may require certain grades in GCSE English language and mathematics. The skills learned in those subjects will be most valuable when studying psychology, as also will the skills learned studying sciences at GCSE level.

However, experience tells us that gaining good grades at GCSE, though certainly useful, is not the main factor in gaining A grades at A-level. What is essential is a desire and motivation to succeed and a necessary part of that desire and motivation is developing and maintaining high levels of self-worth, confidence and persistence.

Every successful person, in whatever walk of life, be it sport, business or study, fails. Indeed failure is an important part of learning. Through failure we can identify what we need to do to improve our learning, then create ways of achieving these new learning aims and finally put these strategies into practice to achieve such aims. That is persistence — not giving up when things don't go right, but instead coming back stronger with your motivation, self-worth and confidence intact.

An A-grade student therefore needs to have high levels of self-honesty — being able to perceive your strengths and use them fully, but also to acknowledge your failings, your weak areas, so that you can create and put into practice strategies to improve these weaknesses so that they become strengths.

To achieve and hone the skills necessary for success, which we are defining here as gaining a grade A, will take time and effort. The aim of this book is to help you develop such skills over the duration of your A-level course. Each chapter focuses on one of the skills necessary to attain a grade A. In each chapter we examine what these skills are, what contributions they make to the studying of psychology and, probably most importantly, how you can develop these skills and use them in your studying of the subject and your successful sitting of the exams.

There is a small variation between different years and different exam boards, but generally about 18% of A-level psychology students will achieve a grade A and about 9% an A*. And, although again there will be small variations between different years and exam boards, you will need to attain about 67% of the available marks for a grade A, and about 75% of the available marks for an A*.

> **! Common pitfall**
>
> Do not allow your confidence and self-worth to be shattered the first time you get an answer wrong or fail to complete an excellent piece of work. Instead try to see such experiences as opportunities to help you identify ways of becoming a better student.

The assessment objectives

In all the four A-level science subjects (physics, chemistry, biology and psychology), the examination marks are divided up by three types of assessment objectives: AO1, AO2 and AO3. Assessment objectives and the proportion of marks awarded for each are not determined by the exam boards, but by a government body: the

Office of Qualifications and Examinations Regulation (Ofqual). Gaining a grade A does not require you to achieve a certain amount of marks for each assessment objective; instead you will be graded on your overall mark. However, to gain a grade A, you will probably need a good proportion of the marks in all three assessment objectives. Therefore you will need to know what skills each one represents in order to formulate strategies to increase your abilities in all these assessed areas.

AO1: knowledge and understanding

AO1 involves demonstrating your knowledge and understanding of research studies, scientific ideas, processes, techniques and procedures. AO1 comprises 30–33% of the marks at A-level. AO1 questions are identified by command words such as 'outline', 'describe' and 'identify'.

Annotated example 1

One explanation of memory is the multi-store model (MSM), which is a cognitive theory that sees memory as comprising a series of stores between which information flows. There are three stores: the sensory register, short-term memory and long-term memory.

This is an AO1 answer, as it describes how the MSM explains memory. It demonstrates the student's knowledge and understanding of the model.

Annotated example 2

Jenness (1932) performed an experiment into informational social influence (ISI) that aimed to investigate whether individual judgements of jelly beans in a jar were influenced by discussion in groups. Male and female participants made individual, private estimates of how many jelly beans were in a jar, then discussed their estimates in groups in order to arrive at group estimates, and then finally made individual, private estimates again. It was found that individuals' second private estimates moved closer to their group estimates than their first private estimates. This was greater among females than males.

This is AO1, as it describes the aim of Jenness's study into conformity.

This is AO1, as it describes the procedure of the experiment.

This is AO1, as it outlines the results of Jenness's study.

AO2: application of knowledge

AO2 involves the application of your knowledge and understanding of scientific ideas, processes, techniques and procedures: in a theoretical context, in a practical context and when handling qualitative and quantitative data. AO2 comprises 30–33% of the marks at A-level. AO2 questions are identified by the inclusion of stimulus material in questions that you have to refer to in your answers.

Annotated example 3

> From the scenario above, it can be seen that Mhaira can ride her surfboard without thinking how to do it, as it involves her procedural long-term memory, a type of LTM for performing specific actions that require little conscious processing. However, she finds it much more difficult to remember the answers to her psychology test, as this involves semantic long-term memory, a type of LTM for meanings, understandings and other concept-based information, which requires cognitive processing during their encoding in order for them to be recalled.

This is AO2, as it involves applying knowledge and understanding of types of long-term memory to a given scenario about a girl called Mhaira who can ride her surfboard without having to think how to do it, but has to think quite hard in order to answer questions in a psychology test.

Annotated example 4

> A suitable null hypothesis for the above study would be that there will be no difference in the number of items recalled from a list between participants who are presented with and recall the items in the same room, and participants who are presented with the items in one room, but recall them in another room.

This is AO2, as it is a null hypothesis constructed from information provided about a specific study, in this instance a study testing whether forgetting is in any part due to retrieving information in a different context to that in which it was coded. The answer applies the independent variable (IV) and dependent variable (DV) identified from the scenario, to create a suitable null hypothesis.

AO3: analysis, interpretation and evaluation

AO3 involves analysing, interpreting and evaluating scientific information, ideas and evidence, including in relation to issues of making judgements and reaching conclusions, and developing and refining practical design and procedures. AO3 comprises 36–38% of the marks at A-level. AO3 questions are identified by command words such as 'evaluate', 'analyse' and 'compare'.

Annotated example 5

> One strength of the MSM is that it is supported by a wealth of research evidence. For example, Murdock (1962) reported that words at the beginning and end of a list were recalled better than those in the middle, as those at the beginning had been rehearsed and transferred to the long-term memory store (the primacy effect), while those at the end were still in the short-term memory store (the recency effect), which supports the existence of separate short-term and long-term memory stores.

This is AO3, as it provides an evaluation of the MSM, in this instance of the research evidence that supports the model.

Annotated example 6

This is AO3, as it provides a conclusion through analysis of what the findings suggest.

> The findings of Jenness's study demonstrate how individuals seek information from others as to how to respond in ambiguous and novel situations due to a desire to be correct, which may have evolutionary survival value in keeping people safe. The study though tells us nothing about why people conform in non-ambiguous situations to obviously wrong answers. The findings may also suggest normative social influence (NSI), as well as informational social influence (ISI), as participants' second individual estimates may have moved towards their group estimates due to a desire for acceptance (NSI) rather than a desire to be correct (ISI).

This is AO3, as it evaluates the study through criticising what the results don't explain.

This is AO3, as it analyses the results to suggest an alternative explanation, that of NSI as well as ISI.

The key skills an A-grade student needs

Quantitative skills

Ofqual has determined that 10% of the available marks for A-level psychology should assess mathematical skills. The mathematical skills that you will require will generally be ones that you have already learned at GCSE (see Chapter 1). Your psychology course should present you with opportunities to practise and hone these skills, especially in relation to specific psychological contexts and examples. Mathematical skills don't always involve calculations; they can also involve detailing or evaluating mathematical principles that apply to a psychological context.

Chapter 1 focuses on the broad quantitative skills needed for A-level psychology, and includes strategies that you can use to improve your performance in handling mathematical skills, as well as some opportunities to apply these skills.

Reading and note-taking skills

Studying for your A-level psychology course will inevitably involve a lot of reading and note-taking. Usually this occurs in the form of reading and making notes on material from psychology textbooks, generally ones that have been specifically written for the particular exam board specification you are studying. However, reading and note-taking can take in many other sources too, like magazine and newspaper articles, or even reports of specific psychological investigations.

Gaining a grade A won't be dependent though on reading a certain amount of material or making endless notes. What will be important is your *selection* of relevant reading material and how you use this material to develop the skills necessary for success. Equally important are the *means* by which you make notes — generally in ways that improve your knowledge and understanding, but also in ways that organise information so that it relates specifically to the different assessment objectives.

Better students tend to read and make notes from more than one source, as this helps to develop a deeper understanding of the topics and gives more opportunities to use the comparing and contrasting skills needed in assessed answers.

Chapter 2 concentrates on the best ways in which to select and read material, and how to effectively and efficiently organise your material in the form of note-taking.

Writing skills

In your psychology exams, you will be asked different types of questions that will require different types of writing skills to answer them. There is a real art to doing this effectively and many an excellent student, in terms of ability, motivation and hard work, has underachieved solely because their writing skills in the exams were found wanting.

Therefore, Chapters 3 and 4 explore the methods and means of developing such skills. This will involve identifying the different types of question and their requirements and then applying the necessary writing skills in the most effective manner. Chapter 4 will consider in detail the writing skills required for extended response/ essay-type questions.

Practical skills

Psychology is a scientific subject built on research and 25% of the marks in the exams will be for questions based on research methods (including the 10% that assess mathematical skills). Other marks will also be awarded for describing and evaluating relevant research studies when answering questions based on psychological topics.

To gain an A grade, you will need to not only know about psychology, but also to be a psychologist from a practical perspective. Therefore you will need to develop your practical research skills in order to gain a deeper knowledge and understanding of the subject in a way that will benefit you when answering exam questions that relate to research.

There will be opportunities in Chapter 5 to develop your practical skills, through the planning, conducting and writing up of regular mini-practicals based on the topics you are studying, and to learn how best to use the knowledge and understanding gained from such mini-practicals when answering examination questions.

Study skills

Aside from reading, note-taking and writing skills, there are other study skills that will be important in your pursuit of a grade A. These include the organisation and management of your studies in terms of time allocation, short-term and long-term planning, development of critical thinking skills and revision techniques.

Generally, a grade-A student is an independent learner who is more self-organised and self-managed than other students and there are strategies that you can learn and utilise to help you achieve this. You will also need to develop higher-order critical thinking skills, especially in the pursuit of AO3 marks, and again, there are ways and means of developing such skills.

Revision is not something that is just put into action immediately before an exam; instead it should be an essential element of your studies that you use throughout your course. In Chapter 6, effective ways of revising will be outlined, with opportunities to practise and develop such skills. There will however be additional focus on the concentrated period of revision that occurs immediately before your exams, in terms of how to organise and use this time most effectively.

You should know

> **The qualities that distinguish an A-grade student.**
> **What assessment objectives are, and the differences between the different types of assessment objectives.**
> **What key skills an A-grade student should possess: quantitative, reading, note-taking, writing, practical and study skills.**

1 Quantitative skills

The mathematical skills required

Quantitative research involves psychological studies that produce numerical data (data in the form of numbers) and require statistical analysis. The majority of contemporary psychological studies involve quantitative research and the quantitative skills you will need to develop involve those centred on:

→ describing and explaining quantitative research methods

→ the application of quantitative research methods

→ analysing and evaluating quantitative research methods

→ the production and analysis of quantitative data

Of the marks available in the examinations, 10% will be for questions relating to mathematical skills, though the quantitative skills you will be required to demonstrate will not just involve numerical calculations, but will also involve knowledge of the principles and concepts that underpin quantitative research. You may be required to describe such knowledge, as well as providing analysis and evaluation of it, often by applying your answers to given scenarios.

There shouldn't really be any need for you to learn new mathematical skills; instead the requirement will be for you to learn how to *apply* the mathematical skills you already have to psychological topics, in terms of quantitative research. Examples of the mathematical skills required for the exam are shown in Table 1.1.

Table 1.1 Mathematical skills assessed in A-level psychology

Mathematical skill	Example
Arithmetic and numerical computation	
Recognise and use expressions in decimal and standard form	Converting data in standard form from a results table into decimal form in order to construct a pie chart
Use ratios, fractions and percentages	Calculating the percentages of cases that fall into different categories in an observation study
Estimate results	Commenting on the spread of scores for a set of data, which would require estimating the range
Handling data	
Use an appropriate number of significant figures	Expressing a correlation coefficient to two or three significant figures
Find arithmetic means	Calculating the means for two conditions using raw data from a class experiment
Construct and interpret frequency tables and diagrams, bar charts and histograms	Selecting and sketching an appropriate form of data display for a given set of data
Understand simple probability	Explaining the difference between the 0.05 and 0.01 levels of significance
Understand the principles of sampling as applied to scientific data	Explaining how a random or stratified sample could be obtained from a target population
Understand the terms mean, median and mode	Explaining the differences between the mean, median and mode and selecting which measure of central tendency is most appropriate for a given set of data; calculating standard deviation
Use a scatter diagram to identify a correlation between two variables	Plotting two variables from an investigation on a scatter diagram and identifying the pattern as a positive correlation, a negative correlation or no correlation
Use a statistical test	Calculating a non-parametric test of differences using the data from a given experiment
Make order of magnitude calculations	Estimating the mean test score for a large number of participants on the basis of the total overall score
Distinguish between levels of measurement	Stating the level of measurement (nominal, ordinal or interval) that has been used in a study
Know the characteristics of normal and skewed distributions	Being presented with a set of scores from an experiment and being asked to indicate the position of the mean (or median, or mode)
Select an appropriate statistical test	Selecting a suitable inferential test for a given practical investigation and explaining why the chosen test is appropriate
Use statistical tables to determine significance	Using an extract from statistical tables to say whether or not a given observed value is significant at the 0.05 level of significance for a one-tailed test
Understand measures of dispersion, including standard deviation and range	Explaining why the standard deviation might be a more useful measure of dispersion for a given set of scores, e.g. where there is an outlying score
Understand the differences between qualitative and quantitative data	Explaining how a given qualitative measure (e.g. an interview transcript) might be converted into quantitative data
Understand the difference between primary and secondary data	Stating whether data collected by a researcher dealing directly with participants is primary or secondary data

Mathematical skill	Example
Algebra	
Understand and use the symbols: $=, <, \ll, \gg, >, \propto, \sim$	Expressing the outcome of an inferential test in the conventional form by stating the level of significance at the 0.05 level or 0.01 level by using symbols appropriately
Substitute numerical values into algebraic equations using appropriate units for physical quantities	Inserting the appropriate values from a given set of data into the formula for a statistical test, e.g. inserting the N value (for the number of scores) into the chi square formula
Solve simple algebraic equations	Calculating the degrees of freedom for a chi square test
Graphs	
Translate information between graphical, numerical and algebraic forms	Using a set of numerical data (a set of scores) from a record sheet to construct a bar graph
Plot two variables from experimental or other data	Sketching a scatter diagram using two sets of data from a correlational investigation

Source: Ofqual (2014) *GCE AS and A level regulatory requirements for biology, chemistry, physics and psychology*, Department of Education.

How the mathematical skills are assessed

Questions assessing mathematical skills will involve the AO1, AO2 and AO3 assessment objectives.

AO1 questions

AO1 marks are available for describing and explaining quantitative research methods to show your knowledge and understanding of them. Generally, a greater level of accurate detail and a greater clarity in your descriptions and explanations will show a deeper level of understanding.

Therefore, you should be able to describe in sufficient detail the quantitative research methods listed on your exam board's specification, in such a way as to show full understanding of what is being described. This can often be achieved by giving relevant detail and examples.

The difference between...

A-grade students generally show more relevant detail in answers requiring AO1 content than other students. This helps to show their greater depth of knowledge.

Examples of AO1 questions include:

→ Name a measure of dispersion. (1)

→ Explain in what circumstances the standard deviation would be preferred as a measure of dispersion. (3)

→ Explain how a psychologist could use systematic sampling to allocate 15 participants into 5 groups. (3)

→ Explain two reasons for selecting the sign test when subjecting data from a study to statistical analysis. (4)

→ In what ways can the use of primary data improve an investigation? (3)

✓ Exam tip

Use the number of marks available for a question as an indicator of how much detail is required in your answer. As a rule of thumb, for a 2-mark question, 1 mark will be earned by providing a valid point and the second mark by elaborating (providing detail) about the point that communicates understanding. If the question is worth 3 marks, further elaboration, or provision of a valid example, is an effective way of gaining the third mark.

> ! **Common pitfall**
>
> Rather than providing descriptions and explanations, as required by AO1 questions, students often provide evaluation instead, for example in the form of strengths and weaknesses. Such answers are irrelevant and generally occur because students fail to identify the command words in a question that inform you what type of answer is required.

Annotated example 1.1

What is meant by psychologists finding the results of a study to be significant at p < 0.05? (2)

This is an AO1 question, as it requires you to describe your knowledge about the significance of findings at the 5% level.

The first sentence makes a valid point about what significant findings are and earns a mark.

It means that a researcher can conclude that the results are beyond the boundaries of chance. With a 0.05 significance level there is a 95% certainty that this is so.

The second sentence provides relevant elaboration (detail), in this case explaining specifically what a 0.05 significance level is.

The answer has knowledge (provided in the first sentence) and understanding (provided in the second sentence) and easily gains both available marks.

Annotated example 1.2

Explain how a questionnaire could be assessed for test-re-test reliability. (3)

This an AO1 question, as it requires you to outline your knowledge regarding how the test-re-test method is used to assess reliability.

To assess a questionnaire for test-re-test ability, the same participants would have to complete the questionnaire on at least two occasions. Each participant's score from their first attempt would be correlated with their score from their second attempt, by plotting these scores on a scattergram. The scores would then be subjected to a test of correlation, such as Spearman's rho, and if a significant positive correlation was found, the questionnaire could be said to have test-re-test ability.

There are 3 marks available for this question and the answer relates, in separate sentences, three valid steps to establish test-re-test ability. The answer therefore successfully addresses the demands of the question and thus earns all 3 available marks.

Activity

On your exam board's website you will find practice papers and mark schemes for your A-level psychology course (you may have to get your teacher to help you access these). Look at the practice papers and see if you can identify which questions concern the description and explanation of quantitative research methods. Before having a go at answering one of these questions, identify the command words that tell you what kind of answer is required and ensure you know how many points or how much elaboration is required. You can check your answer by reference to the mark scheme.

AO2 questions

AO2 marks are available for applying your knowledge of quantitative research. This involves applying relevant knowledge to given scenarios, for example, data relating to specific research studies. Most exam questions concerning quantitative research will be AO2 ones. Some may require you to carry out calculations and these may be based on data presented in tables or graphs, or on aspects of statistical procedures. All exam boards allow students to use a calculator to make such calculations in the exam. Remember, though, that some AO2 questions will be based on the mathematical principles underlying research rather than just requiring mathematical calculations to be made.

The best way to prepare for AO2 questions based on quantitative research methods is to ensure that you have a solid working knowledge of quantitative research methods and that you regularly practise these types of questions. Indeed, you will need to regularly practise them, as they can occur in exam questions on any topic on any of the exam papers.

✓ Exam tip

In application questions where numerical calculations are required, ensure that you show your calculations. Marks will generally be available for this and by doing so, you will be showing your understanding of the required mathematical techniques.

! Common pitfall

Students often give the correct answer, but fail to relate the answer to the given scenario. For example, you may have correctly identified a positive correlation, but may not have explained it in terms of the specific co-variables in the question — for instance that attractiveness ratings between partners in romantic heterosexual relationships are similar, supporting the matching hypothesis that relations are formed between partners of equal physical attractiveness. Instead, you might have explained that as the value of one co-variable increases, so does the value of the second co-variable. However, this doesn't address the application part of the question and you would probably only gain half the marks available.

Annotated example 1.3

A team of researchers decided to investigate whether using female-orientated items would affect recall of such items between males and females. 20 female-orientated items were presented on a tray to 20 male and 20 female participants for 30 seconds each and were then covered up. Participants then had 1 minute to recall as many items as possible. The mean recall scores are shown in the table. What conclusions might the researchers draw from the data in the table? (4)

Mean recall scores for males and females on a test of female-orientated items

	Males	Females
Mean	11.1	17.2
Standard deviation	1.30	3.54

This is an AO2 question, as it requires you to present a valid conclusion drawn from findings relating to a given example.

> Females will perform better than males on tests of memory when the items to be recalled are ones that are more familiar or of more interest to females than males. Also, the performances of male participants on a memory test involving female-orientated items are less varied and spread out than female participants on the same test.

The word 'conclusions' is used in the question and so you need to present more than one conclusion (however detailed it is) to access all the available marks. Always read the question carefully so you can use the wording to identify exactly what kind of answer is required.

Two types of score are presented in the table — mean score and standard deviation — and the student here sensibly uses them both and thus satisfies the demands of the question to make more than one conclusion. The first conclusion (drawn from the mean scores) generalises, accurately, what the scores suggest about the memory abilities of men and women. The second conclusion (drawn from the standard deviation scores) accurately explains how there is less dispersion among male than female scores.

This question is marked out of 4, and the final mark will be probably determined by the examiner referring to mark levels/bands that describe what qualities should be present in an answer to earn varying amounts of marks. For the highest level, the conclusions drawn would have to be 'accurate and generally well detailed and coherent'. As this is so for both conclusions made here, 4 marks would be earned. There is no need to refer directly to the scores given in the table, as the question does not require it. However, such a reference could be made in order to justify the conclusions being made. Full marks were gained here without the need to do so, which shows there is often more than one way to earn full marks in a question.

Annotated example 1.4

A team of researchers wanted to see if teenagers had a preference for selecting a sweetened drink or a non-sweetened drink. 20 teenagers sampled a sweetened drink and a non-sweetened drink and gave their preference if they had one. Preferences can be seen in the table.

For significance, the value of the less frequent sign is equal to or less than the value in the table.

Participants' preferences for sweetened and non-sweetened drinks

Participant	Preferred sweetened drink	Preferred non-sweetened drink	Had no preference
1		✓	
2		✓	
3	✓		
4		✓	
5	✓		
6	✓		
7	✓		
8		✓	
9	✓		
10		✓	
11	✓		
12	✓		
13			✓
14	✓		
15			✓
16	✓		
17	✓		
18			✓
19	✓		
20	✓		

(a) Calculate the sign test value of *s* for the data in the table above and explain how your answer was reached. **(2)**

This is an AO2 question, as it requires you to calculate a sign test using data supplied from a given scenario.

> The value of *s* is 5. This is because out of the 17 preference scores (with the no preference scores disregarded), the least frequently occurring sign is 5.

The sign test is calculated correctly and the procedure by which this was arrived at is fully explained. 2 out of 2 marks are awarded.

(b) Refer to the critical values in the table below, to explain whether or not the value of s calculated in part (a) is significant at the 0.05 level for a two-tailed test. (2)

N	0.005 (one-tailed) 0.01 (two-tailed)	0.01 (one-tailed) 0.02 (two-tailed)	0.025 (one-tailed) 0.05 (two-tailed)	0.05 (one-tailed) 0.10 (two-tailed)
16	2	2	3	4
17	2	3	4	4
18	3	3	4	5

This is an AO2 question, as it requires you to apply data from a given scenario to decide whether the value of s is significant or not.

> The value of s is not significant at the 0.05 level for a two-tailed test. This is because the critical value is 4 and as the observed value (5) is higher than this, it is not significant at this level.

A correct answer (not significant) is given and the reason for this is fully explained in terms of the observed value and the critical value, therefore both available marks are earned.

Activity

Try this question to test your application of knowledge.

A researcher got 10 male and 10 female participants to play an aggressive video game and then complete a test of arousal, scored out of 10, where 10 was 'very aroused' and 1 was 'not aroused'. Participants' scores are recorded in the table.

Male and female levels of arousal after playing an aggressive video game

Participant	Male scores	Female scores
1	9	7
2	7	7
3	7	6
4	6	7
5	8	5
6	3	3
7	6	4
8	8	6
9	7	5
10	9	2

(a) Using the data in the table above, draw conclusions about levels of male and female arousal after playing aggressive video games. (3)

(b) Select an appropriate graph for displaying the data in the table above. Explain one reason for your choice of graph. (3)

(c) Select an appropriate statistical test for analysing the data in the above table. Give two reasons for your choice of test. (3)

(d) The mean score for arousal was 7.0 for males and 5.2 for females. What percentage of males and females scored below their mean scores? Show your calculations. (4)

(e) Describe how the researcher could have used a statistical test to establish concurrent validity of the test of arousal. (4)

Activity

In exam questions you will often be asked to engage with quantitative scenarios concerning experimental design, levels of data and choice of statistical tests. Therefore to help you maximise your marks with such questions, draw up a list of the possible non-parametric and parametric statistical tests (as outlined in your exam board's specification) and memorise them in terms of which type of experiment they relate to (independent groups, repeated measures and matched participant designs), what level of data they require, and whether they are for use with experimental or correlational designs.

The difference between...

With quantitative research questions that require AO2 content, A-grade students generally show more application than other students. Their answers are more orientated to the scenario/information given in the question, which displays their skill in relating their psychological knowledge to given examples.

AO3 questions

AO3 marks are available for analysing and evaluating quantitative research methods. This involves a consideration of relevant strengths and weaknesses (evaluation) and the drawing and exploration of conclusions (analysis and interpretation). Often these types of questions will also have an AO2 element to them, as some available marks will be conditional on applying the answer to a given scenario.

Generally, the greater the level of elaboration shown in answering these types of questions, the greater will be the number of available marks gained.

AO3 questions require higher-level study skills to answer at the top level, and such answers should have a level of sophistication about them, which reflects a deeper understanding of the subject. These are skills you can gain over time by practice.

Examples of AO3 questions include the following:

→ Explain one strength of using quantitative data in psychological research. (2)

→ Explain one limitation of using quantitative data in psychological research. (2)

> ✓ **Exam tip**
>
> Some AO3 questions require a certain number of points to be made to gain the marks available. Identify from the wording of the question precisely how many points you need to make and then do so with clarity.

→ Explain one strength and one limitation of using the range as a measure of dispersion. (4)

→ Explain in what circumstances, with a set of data, the median would be preferred to the mean. (3)

> **! Common pitfall**
> •
> A common error in answering AO3 questions is not providing enough elaboration (detail). Use the mark allocation for the question as an indicator of how much detail is required.

Annotated example 1.5

Explain one strength and one limitation of using the mean as a measure of central tendency. (2+2)

This is an AO3 question, as it requires you to evaluate the mean in terms of a strength and a weakness of the measure.

The first sentence of each paragraph presents a valid point (a strength and a weakness), gaining 1 mark each.

> One strength of the mean is that it uses all of the scores in a set of data in its calculation. This means that it is the most accurate measure of central tendency, as the mode and median do not use all scores in their calculation.
>
> One weakness of the mean is that it may not actually be representative of any actual score in a set of scores. For example, in the set of scores 1, 2, 6, 7 the mean is 4, but 4 is not actually represented as one of the scores.

The second sentence in each paragraph then elaborates on the point, showing the student's understanding of what is being presented, gaining a second mark for each, thus 2+2 marks are gained overall.

Annotated example 1.6

Explain in what circumstances, with a set of data, the mode would be preferred to the mean. (2)

This is an AO3 question, as the answer is gained by evaluating the mode and the mean, in terms of their strengths and weaknesses.

> The mode is preferred in a set of data when categorical data is used and the researcher wants to know which is the most common category in the data.

A correct answer is given and explained sufficiently to gain both available marks.

Activity

So that you get into the habit of automatically producing answers that fully answer these types of questions, try and write some evaluation/analysis-type questions of your own that require elaboration and then answer them in sufficient detail (or swop questions with a classmate and answer each other's). For example, 'Explain one limitation of using standard deviation as a measure of dispersion.' Your answer would require you to give a valid limitation and explain why it is a limitation.

The difference between...

With quantitative research questions that require AO3 content, A-grade students generally elaborate their answers more than other students. This allows them to access a greater proportion of the available marks, because such elaboration displays a deeper understanding of evaluative material.

Take it further

Use the internet to search for the published reports of classic research studies (the ones featured in your exam board's specification). Have a close look at the results section of the reports, and the appendices that relate to quantitative skills, such as the presentation of raw data and the details of any statistical test analysis. This will help you to develop a greater knowledge and understanding of the importance of quantitative research skills in psychology.

You should know

> **What quantitative research is.**
> **The mathematical skills necessary for A-level psychology.**
> **How AO1, AO2 and AO3 questions assess your mathematical skills.**
> **How much detail to include in your answers to AO1 questions on quantitative research methods.**
> **How to relate your answers to aspects of given scenarios when answering AO2 questions on quantitative research methods.**
> **How to elaborate on your points in your answers to AO3 questions on quantitative research methods.**

2 Reading and note-taking skills

Learning outcomes

> Develop your reading skills in order to learn more effectively
> Understand how to use your textbook and other source materials effectively
> Develop your metacognition (the awareness and understanding of one's own thought processes)
> Develop your note-taking skills to actively process your learning
> Understand the meaning of the different command words

The development and application of appropriate reading skills throughout your A-level psychology course is an essential requirement for achieving at the highest level in the exams. Reading skills are also imperative for studying at degree level, so gaining and honing these skills now will be time well spent, particularly if you wish to progress on to university. A-grade students tend to spend a considerable amount of time studying independently outside of the classroom (as you would also do at university) and much of this involves reading from a variety of sources. Unless the requisite reading skills are developed, it will not be possible to study independently in a manner that will enhance your chances of exam success.

When starting an A-level course, students tend to rely on their tried-and-tested study methods, including their reading skills, learned from their GCSE subjects. However, such methods may be inappropriate at this level and indeed may hinder your studies, helping to create a 'glass ceiling' or barrier to you advancing your abilities as an A-level psychology student.

In this chapter, we look at how to select and use appropriate reading materials in the most effective manner. The focus will be on the development of your metacognitive skills, so that you have a greater awareness and comprehension of your thought processes when reading. We also look at how you can incorporate reading with note-taking. Indeed, reading and note-taking, when done effectively, should be seen as one collective skill, rather than as two separate ones.

Aiming for an A in A-level Psychology

Reading skills
Types of reading sources

Part of developing your reading skills is exploring what different reading sources have to offer, including:

→ your main textbook
→ other textbooks
→ scientific journals
→ relevant websites
→ newspaper and magazine articles
→ other associated sources, for example books and magazines on science, philosophy and so on.

Your main textbook

Many schools and colleges provide their students with a main A-level textbook and your teacher will probably have spent time carefully choosing the one they think will serve you best. Having a textbook is recommended, as it will probably be your principal resource in studying for your A-level. However you come by a textbook, try to check the contents list against the specification for your exam board. All exam boards make their specifications available on their websites, so you can check that the book you intend to use matches the current specification. All exam boards' specifications have changed quite recently, so you don't want to end up using a book, however good, which matches an old specification that is no longer being examined.

Good textbooks tend to have extra features in addition to the descriptions of relevant theories and studies. For example, they may contain extension activities for more able students, comprehension-style exercises, exam-style questions and advice on how to attempt them, and may differentiate the text in terms of descriptive and evaluative sections. There may also be exercises based around research, such as suggestions for mini-practicals, and questions based on research methods. Such additional features will serve those looking to attain a grade A very well, as they will provide opportunities to reinforce your learning, further your knowledge and understanding, and develop critical skills that will be vital in securing high-level AO2 and AO3 marks in your final exams.

> ✓ **Exam tip**
>
> Don't just use your textbook as a source of information — use the exercises to develop not just your knowledge and understanding, but also your critical faculties and your ability to answer exam questions.

Other textbooks

Although it is highly recommended that you use one exam-board-specific textbook as your primary source for your A-level studies, it is also advisable that you periodically use other relevant textbooks too. Experienced examiners can quickly tell, when marking a student's exam paper, exactly which textbook they have been using and this can have the effect of limiting the marks that will be awarded. Students who have used more than one textbook are often able to construct answers that have a greater depth and sophistication to them. This is especially true when contrasting and comparing theories or studies, as different textbooks may illuminate and explore such theories and studies in different ways. This allows students to present answers with a greater scope that will reflect well on their level of understanding and critical awareness. This then permits examiners to award higher levels of marks.

Check with your teacher to see what other textbooks are available for you to use. Your school and local library may also have appropriate books that you could use.

> ## ! Common pitfall
> Many students only ever use one textbook and this limits the content they can generate, descriptive and evaluative, in written exam answers. Many students also spend a lot of time memorising passages of text from their textbook and then just regurgitate this in the exam, which can severely limit the marks received.

Activity

See if you can find another textbook for your course other than your main one. Choose a topic, read through it in both books and make a list in bullet-point form of similarities and differences (this can be for both descriptive and evaluative content). This could help form the basis of a much more sophisticated exam answer (especially for essay questions) than just using the one book.

Scientific journals

Psychological knowledge (e.g. theories, models and explanations) is gained from psychologists conducting research studies. Full details of such studies are published in recognised, peer-reviewed journals, and the best way for A-level students to access such journals is via the internet. This includes current, up-to-date issues, as well as older issues. Studies published in journals usually contain more detail than when they are written about in textbooks. So for famous psychology studies (e.g. Milgram's (1963) obedience study), studies that are specifically listed on your exam board's specification, and up-to-date, contemporary studies, the best way to gain knowledge and understanding of them (including critical evaluation) will be to access them in their full form in the relevant scientific journal. Reading studies in this way will also give you a better understanding of the scientific process, which you may be examined on.

Relevant websites

There is a vast amount of invaluable information on the internet which can be used to reinforce and complement your studies, but it is important that you assess whether the information accessed is valid (true), and relevant to your studies.

Your textbook and your teacher will be able to direct you to many appropriate and useful websites. For example, www.simplypsychology.org is one that showcases psychological articles and contains resources for students that will assist learning. Another is www.psychologytoday.com, an American website overseen by the American Psychological Association. Valid websites will refer to peer-reviewed research and will provide references to access such research. Being able to assess the validity of information that you are reading is a critical skill in itself.

Newspaper and magazine articles

Many magazines and newspapers feature psychological articles of interest and these can often supplement your learning or point you towards interesting research or topics that can be further investigated by accessing the relevant scientific journals. Again, care should be taken not to unquestioningly accept as valid the information and conclusions presented in such articles. As your knowledge of psychology and how the discipline functions improves, you should be able to use your developing critical and analytic skills to evaluate the scientific value and validity of what you are reading, so magazine and newspaper articles can be a valuable tool in the development of your critical awareness.

Other associated sources

Top-level psychology students are not going to restrict themselves to reading materials. that are orientated specifically to the subject. Psychology is based on scientific and philosophical foundations, so wider reading that encompasses such material would also be beneficial to your studies.

As an A-level psychology student, you will be expected to have knowledge and understanding of psychological approaches, issues and debates, as well as a solid understanding of the scientific method and principles upon which much of psychology is based (and the philosophies and methods that underpin the non-scientific aspects of psychology too). Therefore books, magazines, websites and so on that have a wider focus, but are related to the psychological topics you will study, will supplement your learning. For example, you might look at publications like *New Scientist*, which many schools and colleges will stock in their libraries.

Take it further

Get into the habit of regularly reading specialist academic psychology magazines. Many schools and colleges have a subscription to the *Psychology Review* magazine, for example, which is orientated towards students studying A-level psychology (if your school doesn't have a subscription, you can take out a private one). There you will find regular features on relevant topics and contributions by leading psychologists, as well as useful exam advice. Go to www.hoddereducation.co.uk/magazines for more information.

The difference between...

In their written work, A-grade students generally display a greater variety of relevant reading than other students. Examiners will be more impressed by students who show evidence of wider reading, as such students are able to give answers with more comparative analysis and a greater breadth of knowledge.

Ways of reading

There are different ways of reading, which broadly break down into *passive reading*, where material is just read through (often simply for pleasure), without any meaningful processing of the information, and *active reading*, where material is processed and analysed while being read. Active reading is a more effective learning technique, but there are occasions when passive reading will be useful too.

Skimming

Skimming is a quick way to read through material. It involves reading text rapidly in order to just get a general idea of the meaning, and it saves time by avoiding unnecessary reading. You can just read introductions, conclusions and headings to get a sense of meaning. Although this method gives a low level of comprehension and a superficial understanding of the material, it is performed to identify and select material that is relevant and which you may wish to read in more detail later on.

Scanning

Scanning is used to identify specific information rapidly within a body of text, for example, a definition of a theory. The technique involves using your eyes to dart quickly across text looking for key words and phrases. It can also involve looking for definitions, highlighted words and phrases, as well as specific information, such as the statistical findings from a study. The technique can be used with diagrams, as well as text.

Intensive reading

Intensive reading involves deeper analysis of text in order to extract from it as much information and meaning as possible. Generally, the technique involves having a set aim in mind, such as documenting the formation of a theory, and exploring the text exhaustively to extract as much relevant detail from it as possible. Any words or phrases that are not understood are looked up in a dictionary, or on the internet. Intensive reading by its very nature requires high levels of focus and cognitive processing. It is best done for small amounts of text, or for limited periods of time, so that attention can be maintained. Thirty minutes is probably the maximum amount of time for which most people can effectively engage in intensive reading. It assists with the retention of information in long-term memory and so lends itself to revision, so that relevant information can be retained and understood and recalled when necessary, for example when sitting tests or exams.

For intensive reading to be effective, reading needs to occur *actively*, not passively. Active reading involves engaging with the text by considering its meaning and analysing and evaluating its validity. Several techniques can be used here, such as highlighting key terms or phrases as and when they occur; composing notes, ideas and questions as reading occurs; writing a brief, concise summary when the text has been read; and making connections from the text to other material that has been read, for instance by comparing and contrasting explanations.

> ✓ **Exam tip**
>
> Scan past exam questions in order to identify the command words. Then do this every time you have a piece of assessed work to do. Eventually this will become an automatic process which will help you to write relevant and appropriate answers in your exams.

Activity

Work with a partner and intensively read some relevant text (maybe from your textbook). Discuss its meaning with each other and ask relevant questions of each other to stimulate deeper processing and analysis. You can read the material individually and silently and then discuss it, or it can be read out aloud by one person and discussed at appropriate points in time.

Extensive reading

Extensive reading involves reading large amounts of text in a relaxed manner, generally for the pure pleasure of doing so. It uses a lot less mental energy than intensive reading and so a larger amount of text can be read and reading can continue for longer — no note-taking or deep analysis is required. It is a passive technique, but one that can be beneficial in helping to develop your vocabulary, especially of psychological terminology, as well as assisting in forming ideas and viewpoints about psychological topics.

Extensive reading, performed in a relaxed manner, can help students to assimilate new material by incorporating the material into existing knowledge and understanding, leading to a deeper and more confident understanding of the material you have been learning. It is not suitable for challenging, difficult-to-comprehend material, as this requires more active forms of intensive reading.

! Common pitfall

Too many students rely solely on extensive reading when reading their textbook. This is not going to help you deepen your knowledge and understanding, nor will it help you prepare for tests or complete assessed pieces of homework. It is much better to use a combination of scanning and intensive reading.

Activity

Use your school or college library to access a specialist psychology magazine, such as *Psychology Today*. Skim read the list of contents to identify a topic relevant to your exam board's specification. Use scanning to see if you can identify what specific information is being featured in the article. Then go back over the article using intensive reading to see what deeper meanings and detail you can extract from it.

Metacognition

Metacognition concerns an awareness and understanding of one's own thought processes — in other words, thinking about how you think. Once you gain an understanding of your personal thought processes, you can begin to comprehend the barriers that exist to advancing your performance as a student, in other words to realise the limitations of your thought processes. This applies very much to the way you read material.

In order to become a better, more effective reader, you need to develop an insight into how you currently read and the ways in which this could be improved. Only then will your understanding and performance as a student be able to improve.

Several tried and trusted reading strategies exist that can be utilised to improve your levels of metacognition:

→ **Reading aloud**. This is an effective strategy for improving your comprehension and analysis of the text as it will help you to consciously monitor and reflect on your learning. Another way of doing this is to read a passage of text and then *think aloud* about what you have just read in terms of what it means, the strength of any evidence presented, what conclusions can be drawn and so on. An important consideration will be to try and identify any limitations in the means by which you are reading, for example, reading text and then having no recollection of it, or reading text without considering its relevance and validity.

→ **Asking yourself questions**. You can do this when you complete your reading, but it is probably more useful, especially with lengthier pieces of text, when used at regular intervals. Have a set list of questions to ask yourself. These will depend on the type of text being read, but they can include such questions as, 'What are the main points being made?', 'Are these points supported by evidence?', 'Are there any parts that are unclear or not understood?', 'What conclusions can I draw from what I have read?', 'What questions/issues can I think of concerning what I have just read?' These questions can be answered out loud, or the answers jotted down as notes (perhaps as sticky notes by the side of the text).

→ **Reading in pairs/small groups**. Here, group members take it in turns to read out loud parts of the text. Other group members then ask the reader questions about what has been read to assess their level of comprehension and analytic abilities — for example, asking them to summarise the main points of what has been read, or asking what evidence has been provided to back up the points being made, and how valid this evidence is. This strategy can be turned around, so that it is the reader who then asks their audience these questions.

→ **Reading to an imaginary audience**. This is an effective strategy as it involves you the learner thinking about and interacting with text from different perspectives: that of the reader of the text and of the audience being read to. It involves imagining yourself reading to a listener, so that your reading has to be clear and slow paced. Get the 'listener' part of you to frame and ask relevant, probing questions, such as 'How do we know that is true?' And then you as the 'reader' have to fully answer such questions. Alternatively, you as the 'reader' can ask you as the 'listener' questions, such as 'What are the key points concerning what I have just read to you and what criticisms can you think of at this point?'

If, at any point in the reading process, problem areas become apparent, these should not be ignored, but identified and concentrated on, as part of the process of identifying weaknesses in metacognition. Strategies should then be applied to eradicate these deficiencies. For example, if while reading aloud to yourself or others, it becomes apparent that you can't recall what was read, then ways of improving your retention should be utilised, such as re-reading the text, re-reading it aloud, highlighting key words/phrases or creating a written summary of the text at regular intervals. In this way it should be possible to identify and address specific issues concerning any weaknesses in your reading. Table 2.1 lists the common weaknesses and suggests strategies to address them.

Table 2.1 Reading weaknesses and strategies to address them

Weaknesses in reading	Strategies to address the weakness
Not being able to recall what was read	Re-read the text, read it out loud, highlight key words/phrases, compile a written summary
Not having full knowledge and understanding of what was read	Identify the key points/meanings, explain the key points/meanings, give examples of your own that show your understanding
Being unable to analyse (draw conclusions from) what was read	Compile a list of conclusions from the text, underline where in the text these conclusions can be drawn from
Being unable to evaluate (identify the strengths and limitations of) what was read	Draw up a table of strengths and limitations identified from the text, underline in the text (using two different colours) where the strengths and limitations occur
An inability to critically assess (ask questions of) what has been read	For each section of text read, jot down a relevant question and/or criticism
An inability to compare and contrast with a similar text (e.g. with other explanations/theories and related research studies)	Place the two texts side by side and read them in unison, jotting down the similarities (comparisons) and differences (contrasts) as you go

Effective reading involves actively engaging with the text and comprehending its meaning and validity. Enhancing your metacognitive awareness by developing your reading skills is essential, as evidence shows that students with low reading comprehension struggle to achieve academically, however well motivated and hardworking they are.

Activity

Read some relevant text to an imaginary audience (e.g. from a psychology magazine or your textbook). You could even do it as different characters using different voices. It will help you to come at the content from different viewpoints, stimulating a deeper processing and comprehension of the information.

The difference between...

A-grade students show greater levels of metacognition in their written work, which reflects their greater reading skills. This shown by their ability to provide incisive summaries and conclusions and to construct analysis that is considered and balanced, exploring all sides of an argument.

Assessing sources

There is a huge amount of source material about psychological topics available. However, not all sources are as valid as they should be, nor as informative and as meaningful as others. Therefore a critical skill to develop is that of assessing sources. This can be achieved in several ways.

Assessing the author

Any credible reading source should identify its creator. Is the author one who is widely known and respected in psychology? If so then the chances are that this is a credible source. You can use the internet to look up details about the author and check if they are a respected psychologist or scientist. If they have any bias towards or against a specific theory, you should be able to identify this and take it into consideration when analysing and evaluating the source. For example, Professor Linda Gottfredson is an eminent psychologist specialising in the field of intelligence and education. However, when checking her credentials, it can be seen that she has a bias towards theories that see intelligence as genetic, and against theories that see intelligence as largely learned. It can also be seen that her research has been partially financed by groups regarded as racist and white supremacist, who have an interest in 'proving' that intelligence is inherited and has a racial element to it. Therefore, the biases in her beliefs should be included in any assessment when reading about her work.

The reasons why the source has been written should also be considered. Is the author merely putting forward their views on a topic? Are they relating some research findings of their own? If so, the text has probably been more considered and thought about during its creation and evidence is provided to back up its claims. However, if the author is instead replying rather angrily to someone's criticism of their work, then the scientific rigour of the piece may be less than it could have been.

Assessing the source

The credibility of a source can be greatly enhanced, or reduced, by considering its origins. If the source is contained within an approved textbook or a peer-reviewed scientific journal, then it is highly likely that the source is credible and trustworthy. If, however, a source is contained within a newspaper or magazine, then the political and philosophical leanings of that publication should be considered. For example, certain newspapers are known for their right-wing or left-wing political leanings and as such will employ authors to write articles that fit their views. It is no surprise that right-wing publications have often featured articles by contributors like Professor Gottfredson, as her viewpoints closely match theirs. Again such biases should be included in any assessment of the material.

Another way of assessing a source is to consider how it is presented in different publications, which may concentrate on and accentuate different features of the material in order to match their different viewpoints, for example, whether a condition such as schizophrenia is genetic or learned in nature. If the source is printed in a book, then it should be possible to find reviews of the book that highlight any shortcomings or biases in the publication.

If a source comes from a website then the ownership and bias of that website should definitely be considered. Sources read from a website should never be accepted as being credible without due consideration, unless the website is widely accepted as one with scientific and unbiased viewpoints.

Activity

Look at a psychology magazine, such as *Psychology Today*, pick an article and use the internet to find out details about the author, especially any beliefs or attitudes they might hold. Then read the article and see if you can identify any examples of the author's beliefs and attitudes within it.

Assessing the content

The style of writing should provide an indication as to the credibility of the source and the more you read, the better you will become in assessing writing styles. Developing an ability to determine what is fact and what is merely someone's opinion is essential in becoming a better learner. For example, if the author is merely stating an opinion or giving an unsubstantiated view, this should quickly become apparent — good indications towards this end are an examination of whether any checkable 'facts' are provided and whether research evidence is quoted which is referenced and therefore also checkable. Is the author giving a one-sided, somewhat biased view or are you being presented with a balanced account that gives different viewpoints with supporting evidence?

Assessing the evidence

This is not something that you were required to do to any great extent at GCSE, but to do well at A-level, it is a very necessary skill to develop. This type of assessment requires an appraisal of the evidence quoted in support or refutation of an explanation, theory, therapy or other claim. The source of the evidence needs to be considered to ensure that it has scientific rigour and is not representing a biased viewpoint. The evidence should be referenced, not only so its source can be examined, but to ensure that it has been reported in its entirety and has not been amended in any way. The conclusions drawn from the evidence should be examined to see that they are logical and fully suggested by the evidence. Are there alternative conclusions that have not been included? It is also important to consider whether any evidence has not been included, especially if such evidence goes against the viewpoint being put forward, as this would suggest that the viewpoint is a somewhat biased and not fully supported one.

Note-taking

The purpose of note-taking

Note-taking is an essential academic skill, but many students do not make notes in an effective manner and indeed some students take notes in ways that actually hinder their learning. How notes are taken should reflect the reason for making them, and the method can vary for different purposes.

What note-taking should never be is an exercise in copying down chunks of text that you have read (or indeed, the words spoken by your teacher). This serves no useful purpose as little if any active processing of the text is occurring. For example, you are not increasing your AO1 skills of knowledge and understanding, nor are you developing your AO3 skills of critical analysis and evaluation.

Increasing numbers of students use a laptop, or similar device, to take notes when reading a text. However, current research suggests that this method is not as effective a learning tool as using pen and paper to take notes. The reasons for this are not yet fully understood, but it is thought that the traditional pen-and-paper method involves more attention and cognitive processing of the text and thus a better understanding and critical awareness of

> **! Common pitfall**
>
> Students often take anything they read at face value. Many articles about psychology on the internet (and to a somewhat lesser extent in many magazines and newspapers) will contain inaccuracies and unsubstantiated personal opinions. These then find their way into students' assessed work where they will attract very little if any credit.

the text. For example, Mueller and Oppenheimer (2014) compared participants making notes while attending a lecture, either on a laptop or by pen and paper and found that:

→ participants scored equally well for recall of facts

→ the pen-and-paper participants scored much better for understanding of ideas and concepts, which suggests they had a deeper understanding of the material

→ the pen-and-paper participants also recalled information more accurately over time, which additionally suggests that they had stronger long-term memories of the information presented in the lecture

(See also Wood et al. (2001) and Carr (2010).)

What note-taking should generally do is to assist in the active processing of material, so that:

(i) a deeper and more lasting understanding occurs

(ii) a meaningful critical awareness of the material, in terms of analysis and evaluation, occurs

Note-taking also 'slims down' material to the pertinent points, making it easier to understand and recall.

How to take notes

When reading text, your notes should reflect the main points or ideas, and provide a summary containing relevant detail. Your note-taking can also help you to organise the material, which will reflect the way it is stored in your memory. Therefore it is often a good idea to put summaries of points into list or table form.

When you come to revising topics (which you should do regularly, not just at the end of your course), you should be able to rely heavily on the notes you have made. These should reflect the knowledge and understanding you have gained, and the different aspects of the topic (facts, conclusions, evaluative points) should be organised into separate sections. The quality of your notes will reflect on how effectively you are organising the information learned into your long-term memory. This will have a huge impact on your recall during the exams and thus ultimately on the marks and overall grade that you will achieve.

One last thing an A-grade student could be doing with their notes is to cross-reference them to other relevant material studied in other topics, as this may form a useful means of evaluating the material currently being learned. For example, you may have been reading, and making notes about, Arthur Jenness's famous 1932 study of informational social influence (ISI), where he found that people's individual estimates of sweets in a jar tended to move towards a group estimate, reflecting how we look to others for guidance as to how to behave in novel or uncertain situations. But you could also cross-reference this to notes you have made elsewhere about the evolutionary approach, as ISI might have an adaptive survival value in helping people to avoid danger by looking to more knowledgeable others as to how to behave in potentially perilous situations.

> ☑ **Exam tip**
>
> It is a good idea to separate your notes into knowledge and understanding (AO1, for example, the description of a theory), and analysis and evaluation (AO3, for example, conclusions and strengths and weaknesses), as these will often be examined separately and so need to be understood as such. A useful trick here is to use one colour of pen for your notes pertaining to descriptions of knowledge, and another colour for your notes pertaining to analysis and evaluation.

> ☑ **Exam tip**
>
> To increase your understanding and critical awareness, and improve your chances of recall, it is a good idea to take the notes you have made and reorganise them further so that they are more concise, coherent and structured. In this way you will be conducting a more meaningful processing of the material being learned. The reorganised notes will also help in your final revision.

Worked example 2.1

Read the following text about the multi-store model of memory. Summarise the text into bullet points in table form, and organise your notes into the following sections:

→ descriptive points (AO1)

→ analytical points (AO2)

→ evaluative points (AO3)

The multi-store model

The multi-store model of memory (MSM) was the first cognitive explanation of memory and created interest in the phenomena that led to much research and subsequent theories. The MSM sees memory as consisting of three storage systems through which information flows. The three storage systems are the sensory register (SR), which holds impressions of vast amounts of information received by the senses for very brief periods; short-term memory (STM), which temporarily holds small amounts of information that are paid attention to for a short time; and long-term memory (LTM), which holds limitless amounts of information transferred from STM for prolonged periods.

The storage systems differ in terms of coding (the means by which information is represented in memory), capacity (the amount of information that can be stored) and duration (the length of time that information can be stored). The model is supported by research evidence and by amnesia cases that indicate STM and LTM use different brain areas and thus are separate stores, as suggested by the model. However, the model is an over-simplified one; evidence suggests there are several different STM and LTM stores. The model also focuses too much on the structure of memory and too little on its processes.

Notes on the MSM

Description of the MSM (AO1)

- *MSM was first cognitive explanation of memory.*
- *Memory consists of three storage systems through which information flows.*
- *The SR stores all sensory information received by the senses very briefly.*
- *STM holds information paid attention to for a short time.*
- *LTM holds lots of information transferred from STM for lengthy periods of time.*
- *The stores differ in terms of coding, capacity and duration.*
- *Coding concerns how information is represented in storage.*
- *Duration concerns how long information is held for in storage.*
- *Capacity concerns how much information is held in storage.*

Analysis of the MSM (AO3)

The MSM is a cognitive explanation, as it focuses on the mental processes active during the memory process.

Evaluation of the MSM (AO3)

Strengths	Limitations
• *The MSM created interest and research into memory that led to subsequent theories.*	• *The model concentrates too much on structure and too little on processes.*
• *The model permits assessment by scientific research.*	• *The model is over-simplified, as there are several types of STM and LTM.*
• *The model is supported by research evidence.*	
• *The model is supported by amnesia cases that suggest STM and LTM are separate memory stores.*	

Activity

Now try summarising this text on the working memory model of memory into appropriate tables as demonstrated above.

The working memory model

The working memory model (WMM) is a cognitive explanation of memory constructed by Baddeley and Hitch (1974). It was inspired by the earlier multi-store model (MSM), but it concentrates only on short-term memory (STM), which it sees as an active store holding several pieces of information simultaneously. Therefore STM is more complex than just being a temporary store for transferring information to LTM. It is called 'working memory', as it concerns information consciously being thought about (worked upon) now. The model is not a replacement for the MSM, but instead is an explanation of memory based upon the MSM.

The central executive (CE) is the component of the model that oversees and co-ordinates the components of working memory. It acts as a filter to determine which sensory information is attended to and allocates information to the relevant slave systems. The phonological loop (PL) is a slave system component that deals with auditory information, while the visuo-spatial sketchpad (VSS) is a slave system component that deals with visual and spatial information. The episodic buffer (EB) is a slave system component that serves as a temporary store of integrated information from the CE, PL, VSS and LTM.

The CE is probably better understood as a component controlling the focus of attention rather than being a memory store, unlike the PL, VSS and EB. Research suggests that different brain areas are associated with different components, such as the pre-frontal cortex being associated with the CE, and this supports the idea of the components being separate systems reflected in the biology of the brain. Research additionally suggests that people have difficulty performing tasks that simultaneously use the VSS (or simultaneously use the PL), but not when doing tasks that simultaneously use the VSS and PL, which suggests they are separate systems with limited capacity. However, little is known about how the main component, the CE, functions and the model does not explain how LTM functions. The addition of the EB in 2000, to address the shortcoming of the model in not explaining where integrated information was being retained, shows how the process of science works in updating explanations in the face of valid criticisms to provide more robust explanations. The model is criticised though for lacking research support that has ecological validity.

Reading exam questions

Probably the most distressing experience that examiners have, and one that is far too frequent, is marking exam answers that are well written, by evidently motivated, skilled and knowledgeable students, but which get very few marks, as they don't answer the actual question on the exam paper. This occurs because of a failure to read exam questions properly. However, there a few simple guidelines to follow that will ensure this never happens to you.

All exam questions contain 'command words', words that inform you about what kind of answer is required. So, every time you have a test, get into the habit of identifying and highlighting the command words in a question. You will of course also have to know what these command words mean — definitions are given in Table 2.2.

Table 2.2 Command words and their meaning

AO1 command words
Calculate — obtain a mathematical answer
Complete — fill in missing information
Define — give the meaning of something
Describe — give a detailed account
Identify — name a specific thing
Outline — give a brief description of
Select — choose a correct option

AO2 command words
Refer to — include information from a given source

AO3 command words
Give — show an awareness of
Explain — give an account of why and how something is so
Evaluate — consider the value or effectiveness of
Discuss — give a balanced account, which will include descriptive (AO1) and evaluative (AO3) content
Assess — judge the importance or quality of
Analyse — break something down into its component parts
Compare and contrast — show the similarities and differences between two things

Exam questions also generally have the number of marks available in brackets after them, for example:

Explain what is meant by informational social influence. (2)

This will give you an idea of how many points need to be written and can help you to write answers that are neither too short nor too long. The number of marks also indicates how much time should be spent writing an answer, and indeed roughly how many words your answer should contain. This is discussed in more detail in Chapter 3, which looks at writing skills.

The difference between...

A-grade students will directly and clearly address the command words in the question and will create sufficient content according to how many marks are available. In contrast, other students will often wander off the question by writing irrelevant content, or too little or too much content.

You should know

> **The importance of reading skills in independent study.**
> **The different types of reading sources available and what they have to offer.**
> **The different ways of reading: skimming, scanning, intensive and extensive reading.**
> **Strategies to improve levels of metacognition and address reading weaknesses.**
> **How to assess reading sources by assessing the author, source, content and evidence.**
> **How to incorporate your reading skills with note-taking.**
> **How to make notes and the pitfalls of making notes electronically.**
> **The role of note-taking in the active processing of learning.**
> **How to read exam questions effectively.**

3 Exam writing skills

Learning outcomes

> Develop your exam writing skills so you are able to write in a clear and concise fashion
> Understand that answers to different types of exam questions have different writing requirements
> Be able to identify the command words so that you know exactly what type of answer is required
> Understand how to write answers that address the three assessment objectives, A01, A02 and A03

Developing your exam writing skills

In Chapter 2 we looked at an important writing skill, that of note-taking. However, writing your exam answers in a certain time period and without recourse to notes or books is probably the most important writing you will do. The examiners will know nothing of your levels of effort and motivation; all they have to assess your worth is the written answers you provide to the exam questions. Therefore, over the 2 years of your course you will need to learn what good writing practice is (and develop it in your own writing), and what poor writing practice is (and eradicate it from your own writing).

Generally, you will need to learn to write in a clear, concise, structured and sufficiently detailed fashion. However, it is important to remember that different types of written answers are required for different types of exam questions. What works for one type of question won't necessarily work for another. So you will also need to learn how to ascertain exactly what sort of answer is required and how long you should spend on it.

In addition, different exam boards have different ways of presenting questions, so ensure that you are familiar with the style of questions your exam board uses. You can download specimen papers and past papers from your exam board's website.

Nobody is born with perfect writing skills, but these can be developed if you focus closely on the feedback your teachers give you when marking your written work. Try and identify what is seen as effective about your written work and continue to do it, but more importantly try and identify what is *not* effective or is missing from your written work and work on these areas. Don't try and correct all your shortcomings in one go; instead try and work at improving one aspect of your written work at a time. When this has been sufficiently mastered, then move on to the next one.

Aiming for an A in A-level Psychology

Remember, you will have sufficient time to develop the required skills in a relaxed and considered fashion.

Answering different types of exam questions

This chapter examines the different types of exam questions and the writing skills required for each. There is some variation between the exam boards, but essentially there are six types of exam questions, each requiring different sorts of answers:

1 **Selection questions** that provide a number of options from which you select the appropriate answer.

2 **Short-answer questions** that require brief answers, generally based on a specific topic area.

3 **Application questions** that require relevant psychological knowledge to be applied to elements of a given scenario.

4 **Research methods questions** that are based on aspects of research methodology.

5 **Research studies questions** that are based on aspects of psychological research studies.

6 **Extended response/essay questions** that require more lengthy responses. (These are considered separately in Chapter 4.)

Activity

Download the specimen exam papers for psychology and their corresponding mark schemes from your exam board's website. Read through the exam papers first to familiarise yourself with the language. Then read through the corresponding mark schemes in order to develop an understanding of what answers should be written (and not written) in response to the different types of questions.

The difference between...

A-grade students demonstrate their awareness of the requirements of different types of exam questions by tailoring their answers to fit. In contrast, other students will often generate a similar type of answer to whatever exam question they are confronted with, which will not give them access to all the available marks.

Selection questions

Selection questions give you information in a list of options from which you have to select the correct or most appropriate answer. Spare options can be left over, so a choice often has to be made between the options. They are considered the easiest type of question to answer, but are often answered poorly, as generally students just haven't attempted enough of them during their course. They come in a variety of forms and can occur on any topic so make sure you practise this type of question regularly for all the topics you study.

Begin by reading the question carefully and identifying the command words. For example, make sure you know exactly how many selections you need to make. Generally the marks available will be an indication — if 2 marks are available, it usually means two

> **! Common pitfall**
>
> Students often fail to read the question carefully enough, and make only one selection when the question asked for two.

choices have to be made. However, you may have to place options in a table, so make sure you fully understand how to do this, for example, by writing the identifying letter in the table.

> ✓ **Exam tip**
>
> When you have finished studying a topic, have a go at creating your own selection questions for that topic. Swop your questions with a classmate and answer each other's. As well as giving you practice in answering these types of questions, writing such questions is a useful form of revision in itself.

Activity

Make a list of all the topics you are studying for your A-level psychology course and collect examples of selection questions for all these topics. You can find examples in the specimen papers and past papers from your exam board's website, or in your textbooks, or alternatively use your own examples.

Annotated example 3.1

Select from the following descriptions to complete the table below concerning types of attachment. One statement will be left over. (2)

A Children are willing to explore, have high stranger anxiety, and are enthusiastic at the return of their caregiver. Caregiver is sensitive to the child's needs.

B Children are willing to explore, have low stranger anxiety, are indifferent to separation and avoid contact with their caregiver on their return. Caregivers often ignore a child's needs.

C Children are unwilling to explore, have high stranger anxiety, and seek and reject contact with their caregiver on their return. Caregivers often show simultaneous opposite feelings and behaviour towards a child.

Types of attachment	Description
Type A – insecure-avoidant	B
Type B – securely attached	A

This is an AO1 question, as it requires you to express your knowledge about attachment types.

The command word here is 'select', which identifies the question as a selection question where choices must be made from the information given to you. There are 2 marks available which indicates that two choices need to be made. The question requires knowledge of Ainsworth's attachment types, which should be shown by correctly working out which of the given descriptions matches Type A and which Type B, and placing these selections in the correct places in the table. The correct choices have been made (description B for Type A and description A for Type B). Description C describes insecure-resistant attachment (Type C) and so is surplus to requirements.

Annotated example 3.2

Place a 'C' next to the two descriptions below that relate to classical conditioning, and an 'O' next to the two descriptions that relate to operant conditioning. One description will be left over. (4)

→ Involves observation and imitation of a model ☐

→ Involves a stimulus becoming associated with a response [C]

→ Involves learning through the consequences of a behaviour [O]

→ Involves the use of reinforcements [O]

→ Can explain the acquisition of phobias [C]

This is an AO1 question, as it requires you to express your knowledge about classical and operant conditioning.

The command word here is 'place', which again identifies the question as a selection question where choices are made from information provided. There are 4 marks available which illustrates that four choices are to be made. The question requires knowledge of learning theory, specifically classical and operant conditioning, which should be shown by placing two letter 'C's and two letter 'O's in the correct boxes, and this has been successfully achieved. The first bullet-pointed description concerns social learning theory and so is surplus to requirements.

Activity

Try these exam-style, selection questions.

1. Match the following descriptions to the types of long-term memory listed in the table below. One description will be left over. (3)

   A Knowing that e-mails are a form of communication between people

   B Knowing how to surf properly

   C Being able to recall someone's address you have just been given by repeating it sub-vocally

   D Knowing that your brother is younger than you

Type of long-term memory	Description
Episodic	
Procedural	
Semantic	

2. From the statements A, B, C and D below concerning definitions of abnormality, place an 'X' next to the two statements that are false. (2)

   A The deviation from social norms definition sees abnormality as a failure to function adequately. ☐

   B The deviation from ideal mental health definition sees abnormality identified by the characteristics and abilities needed to be considered normal. ☐

   C Definitions of abnormality suffer from issues of cultural relativism. ☐

   D The statistical infrequency definition sees behaviours and conditions that are numerically common as being abnormal. ☐

Short-answer questions

Short-answer questions require specific, brief answers, with some elaboration to gain any available additional marks. Some of these questions require description-only (AO1) answers, and some require evaluation-only (AO3) answers — you will need to understand the command words to identify what kind of answer is required.

Activity

Go through examples of short-answer questions from your textbook or exam board's specimen and past papers and work out which ones require AO1 answers (descriptions of knowledge and understanding) and which ones require AO3 answers (showing analysis and evaluation). Make a list of the command words that help you to successfully identify the two different types.

The marks available are an important guide to knowing how much to write. If a question is worth 2 marks, then 1 mark is generally gained by making a relevant point, and the second mark is gained by elaborating sufficiently on the point. Your initial point, to gain the first mark, should show accurate knowledge, while your elaboration, to gain the second mark, should show your understanding of the point made. If a question is worth 3 marks, you will need to make additional elaboration — a relevant example can often achieve this and show your understanding by its selection. A good way to practise this is to write each part of the answer in a different coloured pen, such as blue for the initial point, red for the elaboration of this point and green for the further elaboration. It should be possible then to see exactly where the first, second and third marks are gained.

> ✓ **Exam tip**
>
> Remember to identify the command words and address the requirements of the question. For example, outlining a definition of abnormality when the question actually asks for a strength or a limitation will lose you marks.

Activity

With two classmates, write a short-answer question worth 3 marks and provide an answer worth 1 mark. Pass your question and partial answer to one of your classmates and get them to add in the elaboration, and then pass this to the second classmate who has to provide additional elaboration.

An alternative route to answering short-answer questions is to make several relevant, but different points (if the wording of the question allows separate points to be made). For example, with a question worth 2 marks, you could make two valid, separate points.

The difference between...

With short-answer questions, A-grade students will show a deeper level of understanding by elaborating their points in sufficient detail or making comparisons if required. Other students often fail to elaborate in enough detail to gain all the available marks.

Short-answer questions should be attempted regularly and for all topics studied. Try to aim for a concise and clear writing style. Some students seem to feel that the more they write, the greater the chances they will provide an accurate answer and get the marks available. However, over-descriptive answers often obscure the point being made, giving the examiner an impression that you don't fully understand what you are writing about.

Annotated example 3.3

Describe normative social influence (NSI). (3)

This is an AO1 question, as it requires you to describe your knowledge and understanding of the NSI explanation of conformity. A valid point concerning NSI needs to be made to earn the initial mark, with sufficient elaboration to gain the other two available marks.

A valid point is made about NSI orientating around a need for acceptance, which is sufficient to gain 1 mark.

> Normative social influence concerns a motivational force to be accepted by a group. The best way to achieve this is through agreement with the group, though this involves public but not private agreement so it doesn't necessarily involve real agreement with the group. An example of NSI might be stating that you like the same kind of music as members of a social group, even though you don't really.

The comments about public, but not private agreement involve sufficient elaboration to gain a second mark.

The provision of a relevant example elaborates the answer further by demonstrating an understanding of NSI. (3/3 marks)

Annotated example 3.4

Explain one strength of the multi-store model of memory (MSM). (3)

This is an AO3 question, requiring evaluation in explaining a strength of the MSM.

An initial valid strength of the MSM is stated, which is worth 1 mark.

> One strength of the MSM is that amnesia case studies show support for the explanation. Scoville (1957) reported on the removal of brain tissue from HM in order to treat his epilepsy, which resulted in anterograde amnesia. HM could not make new LTM's, but his old LTM's remained intact, which supports the idea of separate STM and LTM stores, as suggested by the MSM. This was backed up by the case study of Scott Blozan, reported by Rother (2011), who suffered a brain injury that caused retrograde amnesia where he couldn't access old LTM's, but had an unaffected STM that allowed him to make new LTM's.

Two studies are then used as elaboration, showing that brain damage results in damage to either STM or LTM abilities, but not both, which supports the model's idea that STM and LTM are separate memory stores. (3/3 marks)

Activity

Try these exam-style, short-answer questions.

1 Outline the failure to function adequately definition of abnormality. (3)

2 Explain one limitation of the statistical infrequency definition of abnormality. (2)

Application questions

Application questions require you to apply relevant psychological knowledge to the information provided in a given scenario. An example is explaining what informational social influence is by using information drawn from the scenario to support your explanation.

This type of question prevents students from 'off-loading' a pre-prepared answer — something an A-grade student would never do! Many students find application questions difficult at first, but regular practice will make them easy and familiar to deal with, and answering them will become an automatic process. It is important to attempt application questions for all topics studied, as they can appear anywhere in exam papers.

You will need to provide sufficient content to gain all the available marks, so use the number of marks as an indication of how much to write. Some students find the 'PEA' strategy to be effective:

→ **P** — make a relevant point, in terms of psychological knowledge

→ **E** — explain the point to show your understanding of it

→ **A** — apply the point to the question by using the information given in the scenario to support your answer

A good way of checking whether you are getting the balance right between the amount of detailed psychological knowledge and application to the scenario is to use two different coloured pens to write your answer. Use one colour for the psychological information and a different colour for your application.

! Common pitfall

Many students under-perform on application questions — even though they may give top-quality answers in terms of relevance, clarity and detail, they fail to apply their points as they don't use the information in the scenario to support what they are saying. Generally, it won't be possible to attain more than half marks on application questions if you fail to apply your answer. Some students do the reverse — commenting on the information in the scenario, but not detailing the necessary psychological information.

Activity

Practise answering application questions in pairs. One of you makes a point containing relevant psychological knowledge, then you pass the answer to the other person who applies the point to the scenario.

Annotated example 3.5

30-year-old identical triplets Lina, Lily and Leila Lukik represented Estonia in the Olympic marathon in Brazil in 2016. Lina finished 82nd in 2 hours 45 minutes, while Lily was 97th in 2 hours 48 minutes and Leila was 114th in 2 hours 54 minutes.

Use your knowledge of genotype and phenotype to explain why the triplets recorded different times in the Olympic marathon. (4)

This is an AO2 question, as it requires you to apply your knowledge of the relationship between genotype and phenotype to a given scenario, in this instance one about marathon-running identical triplets who perform at different levels.

> Genotype consists of an individual's basic genetic make-up. The triplets were born with identical genotypes, so it might be thought that their performances in the marathon would be identical. Phenotype however is an individual's actual characteristics and abilities that are determined by the interaction of genotype with environmental factors. In other words, phenotype refers to how environmental factors determine how much of an individual's genetic potential is realised. Therefore, the triplets performed differently as their phenotypes are different. For example, Lina may have run faster than Lily and Leila because she experienced a better diet and had trained more effectively than her sisters. Lina and Lily may have outperformed Leila because Leila was injured and so was not able to train fully enough to realise her genetic potential.

The answer here not only shows a sound knowledge of what genotype and phenotype are, and the relationship between them, but applies this knowledge coherently and accurately to the scenario.

As the triplets have an identical genetic make-up it might be expected that they would perform in an equal manner, but the answer shows how phenotypes might differ due to environmental experiences, resulting in different performances. (4/4 marks)

Activity

Try this exam-style, application question.

Dagma, although terrified of rollercoasters, has agreed to go on one. She and her friends are getting on it now. Her heart is pumping fast, she is breathing heavily and can feel sweat trickling down her back. Dagma can even feel the tension in her muscles.

Making reference to the scenario above, explain the flight-or-fight response.   (4)

Take it further

Have a go at creating your own application questions by identifying suitable current news stories, like the one on page 43 about the Estonian female identical triplets who represented their country in the marathon in the 2016 Olympics (and had different finishing times and places).

Research methods questions

Research methods questions are often focused on specific psychological topics, for example memory, but can also be based on general research methods, such as experimental design. More marks are available for research methods questions than for any other topic area, so it is important to know how to answer such questions effectively. Research methods questions are often used to assess your mathematical skills and may require calculations to be made (see Chapter 1).

Research methods questions occur in various forms. They can be short-answer questions, generally worth up to 3 marks, or longer questions, generally worth more than 3 marks. Short-answer questions are marked by reference to mark descriptors (which describe what an answer should contain to get the available marks), so basically you will receive 1 mark for making a valid point and further marks for elaborating on your point. Again, you can practise writing your answers with different coloured pens — blue for the initial point, red for the elaboration of this point and green for the further elaboration. Longer-answer questions will generally be marked by reference to mark bands/levels, with marks awarded for the overall quality of the answer.

Research methods questions can also occur as AO1 questions, for example, 'Explain what is meant by ordinal level data'; as AO2 questions, when application to a given scenario is required (for example, details about a study); and as AO3 questions, for example, 'Explain one limitation of the case study research method.' These are discussed further below.

It is important, therefore, to identify the command words in the question, so that the appropriate answer is given. Make sure you use the number of marks available too, to guide you on how much to write in an answer.

Activity

Use your exam board's specimen and past papers to collect examples of as many research methods questions as possible. Classify these questions as either AO1 (requiring description and understanding of knowledge), AO2 (requiring application to a given scenario) or AO3 (requiring analysis and evaluation). You will be able to do this by identifying the command words within each question. You can check to see if you were correct by looking at the relevant mark schemes.

AO1 questions on research methods

Answers to AO1 questions on research methods involve giving descriptions and explanations of various aspects of research methods. Generally, the greater the level of accurate detail you produce, and the greater clarity there is to your descriptions and explanations, the deeper the level of understanding you show.

Examples of AO1 questions include:
→ Outline the experimental method. (6)
→ Explain what is meant by a confounding variable. (2)
→ Explain what is meant by informed consent. (2)
→ Describe how a random sample would be conducted for a research study. (3)
→ What is meant by an independent variable? (2)
→ Explain what is meant by qualitative data. (2)

Annotated example 3.6

Describe the correlational study method. (3)

This is an AO1 question as it requires you to outline your knowledge of this particular research method.

Research methods questions worth up to 3 marks are generally assessed by reference to mark descriptors and the student here cleverly presents their answer in separate sentences, each one building upon the previous one, adding in more detail along the way.

A correlational study looks for relationships between co-variables. Correlational studies measure both the strength and direction of such relationships. Correlations can either be positive, where, as the value of one co-variable increases (or decreases), so does the other, or negative, where, as the value of one co-variable increases, the value of the other co-variable decreases.

The first sentence makes an accurate general point about the purpose of correlational studies and this gains 1 mark by itself.

The second and third sentences add relevant elaboration, showing depth of knowledge and understanding of the research method. (3/3 marks)

Annotated example 3.7

Explain three ethical issues psychologists should consider when conducting research. (6)

This is an AO1 question, as it requires you to describe your knowledge of three ethical issues that must be considered when research is performed.

> One ethical issue that needs consideration is that of informed consent: potential participants must be given sufficient details of a study so that they can make a considered decision as to whether to take part. A second issue is that of harm: participants should not endure any psychological or physical stress when partaking in a study greater than that of everyday life. A third issue is that of the right to withdraw: participants should be told during the presentation of standardised instructions that they are not obliged to undertake the study and that they can leave at any time they so wish. This includes withdrawing their data after their participation in a study has finished if they so wish.

This is an accurate, coherent and sufficiently detailed answer that includes reference to three ethical issues. The coherence of the answer especially conveys a sound level of understanding of the issues being explained. The answer therefore meets all the requirements to be placed at the top of the highest mark band/level and gains all available marks.   (6/6 marks)

AO2 questions on research methods

Answers to AO2 questions on research methods involve applying relevant knowledge and understanding to given scenarios, for example, aspects of research methods relating to specific research studies.

The key to successfully answering this type of question is to fully engage with the given scenario when presenting an answer. For example, if a question asks you to construct an experimental hypothesis for a given study, it is not creditworthy to merely explain what an experimental hypothesis is, for instance that it looks for a difference in a dependent variable (DV) between two levels of an independent variable (IV), as this, although correct, doesn't engage with the scenario in any way. To be creditworthy, your answer would need to use the actual DV and IV from the study to construct a valid hypothesis.

Application questions should be easily recognisable by identifying the command words in a question, for example 'For this study...'. Examples of AO2 questions include the following:

→ A team of researchers used a stress scale to measure the amount of stress that individual workers at a factory experienced and the number of days that they were off sick over a 6-month period.

(a) Compose a suitable non-directional (two-tailed) hypothesis for this investigation. (2)

(b) Explain how the researchers might have gained a systematic sample for this study. (2)

→ Researchers decided to compare the brain activity of elderly (70-year-old) individuals during sleep with the activity of young adults (18–25-year-olds). They used EEG measurements for the comparison.

Explain why the data gathered from this study may lack reliability and validity. (4)

→ Explain why Harlow's surrogate mother study with monkeys could be considered unethical. (4)

Annotated example 3.8

To test whether forgetting is due to retrieving information in a different context to that in which it was coded, a researcher read a list of words to two groups of participants. Twenty minutes later, one group recalled the list in the same room, while the other group recalled it in a different room.

(a) Compose a suitable null hypothesis for this experiment. (2)

This is an AO2 question, as it requires you to construct a valid null hypothesis by identifying and using the IV and DV in the study.

> There will be no significant difference between the number of words remembered from a list, by participants recalling the words in the same room they were presented in and participants recalling the words in a different room to that they were presented in.

A valid null hypothesis is presented (one that predicts no significant difference) and this is stated coherently in terms of the independent and dependent variables of the study. (2/2 marks)

(b) Explain by reference to the above study what experimental design was used. (2)

This is an AO2 question, as it requires you to apply details of the study to explain which experimental design has been utilised.

> An independent groups design has been used in the study, as each participant only does one condition of the experiment. Participants either recalled the list of words read to them in the same or a different room.

The student successfully explains what an independent groups design is and fulfils the requirements of the question by explaining how the design is utilised in this particular study. (2/2 marks)

Annotated example 3.9

The cognitive interview is designed to improve recall in police interviews. Researchers had some participants perform a fake assault in front of an audience of witnesses who had replied to an advert to take part in the study. Half were interviewed using a standard police interview and half by the cognitive interview technique. The amount of accurate recall was compared.

(a) Identify the independent variable (IV) and the dependent variable (DV) in this study.

(1+1)

This is an AO2 question, as it requires you to recognise what an IV and DV are through the application of them in this specific study.

> The independent variable is whether a participant is interviewed by the standard police interview or by the cognitive interview technique. The dependent variable is the amount of accurate recall from participants.

The candidate shows they fully understand what an IV and DV are by successfully identifying them in the study. (2/2 marks)

(b) Identify one confounding variable that might occur in the above study.   **(1)**

This is an AO2 question, as it requires you to not only know what a confounding variable is, but demonstrate this knowledge through application to the study.

> One confounding variable might be how much sleep participants had last night, as this could affect their concentration levels when watching the fake assault.

The student shows a sound knowledge and understanding of confounding variables by identifying a valid confounding variable for this specific study. Only 1 mark is available, so no further detail is required. (1/1 mark)

(c) Refer to the study to explain what sampling method was used.   **(2)**

This is an AO2 question, as it requires you to apply the content of the study to explain what sampling method has been used.

> The sampling method used was a self-selected sampling method, as participants volunteered themselves for the study by responding to an advert to take part in the study.

The sampling method is correctly identified and the method is coherently explained in terms of participants responding to an advert to volunteer themselves for the study. (2/2 marks)

AO3 questions on research methods

Answers to AO3 questions on research methods involve the drawing and exploration of conclusions (analysis and interpretation), as well as a consideration of relevant strengths and weaknesses (evaluation). In the exam, these types of questions can have an AO2 element to them, as some available marks will be conditional on applying the answer to a given scenario.

Examples of AO3 questions include the following:

→ Explain one strength of the standard deviation measure of dispersion. (2)

→ Explain one strength of the case study method. (2)

→ Explain how a laboratory experiment differs from a natural experiment. (3)

→ Critically evaluate the experimental method. (8)

Annotated example 3.10

Detail the limitations of the peer review process. (6)

This is an AO3 question, as it requires you to evaluate the peer review process (via its weaknesses).

> Peer review might not always be unbiased; the social relationships that develop between individuals in the narrow social world that researchers exist in may affect the reviewers' degree of impartiality and objectivity. Reviewers may even not accept a piece of research as it argues against their own findings in the field; they may even reject research so they can copy the findings and publish them as their own. There is also the accusation that peer review is performed by elite groups of scientists who may resist the publication of revolutionary ideas, even if they appear to be valid. Another form of potential bias in peer review is that reviewers may have links to organisations, such as drug companies, that may be compromised by research being reviewed. For instance, this may affect studies that suggest a certain anti-psychotic drug is harmful, when the reviewer is sponsored by the company producing that drug.

This is a wide-ranging answer, in that several limitations are given, but in sufficient detail, and in a coherent fashion, to convey a sound sense of understanding. Good use is made of an example (that of compromising a drug company), as a form of explanatory elaboration. The answer therefore meets the requirements for the upper level of the top mark level/band. (6/6 marks)

Annotated example 3.11

Explain how primary and secondary data differ from each other. (2)

This is an AO3 question, as it requires you to give a comparative analysis of primary and secondary data.

> Primary data is data collected by a researcher specifically towards a research aim, which has not been published before, while secondary data is data that was originally collected towards another research aim, which has been published before.

A coherent and accurate answer that sufficiently differentiates between the two data types to merit earning both marks on offer. (2/2 marks)

Research studies questions

Research studies questions require answers that focus on describing and/or evaluating research studies. These questions may be about specific studies that are listed in your exam board's specification, or about studies that students choose to comment on, for example, in response to a question that says 'Outline and evaluate a research study of memory'. The questions may focus on a study as a whole or on specific parts of a study, such as its aims or findings.

Questions requiring descriptive answers (AO1) will generally be focused on aims, procedures and findings, while analytical and evaluative questions (AO3) will generally focus on conclusions and strengths and weaknesses, for instance, in terms of methodology and ethical considerations.

Sometimes extended response or essay questions are based on specific studies – these sorts of questions are dealt with in Chapter 4.

As with other types of question, it is important to understand the command words, as they will tell you exactly what kind of answer is required and thus eliminate the chances of you focusing on the wrong aspects of a study, such as providing evaluation when description is required, or stating the aims of a study when the findings are required. Use the number of marks available as a guide as to how much to write, and practise answering these kinds of questions for all the topics that you study.

Examples of research studies questions include the following:

→ Outline the procedures and findings of one or more studies of Romanian orphans. (6)

→ Outline Asch's (1955) study of conformity. (6)

→ Outline how Levine's (2001) study of cross-cultural altruism investigated helping behaviour. (3)

→ Explain two limitations of Ainsworth's (1978) Strange Situation study of attachment. (4)

→ Explain the purpose of using a correlational design for Maguire's (2000) study of taxi drivers. (2)

✓ **Exam tip**

Check your exam board's specification to ensure that you have studied in sufficient detail all the research studies that are listed there. You should know one or two research studies in detail for every topic that you have studied, in order to be fully prepared for your exams.

> ## ! Common pitfall
>
> Students often only use research studies as a form of evaluation, as you would legitimately do when using studies to assess the validity of theories. However, many research studies questions will also require you to describe aspects of a study, such as the aims, procedures and findings.

Activity

For each of your key studies — the ones specifically listed on your exam board's specification, plus one from each topic studied where a study isn't specifically listed — record separately details of (i) the aim(s), (ii) the design, (iii) the procedure, (iv) the findings, (v) the conclusions, and (vi) the evaluative points.

It would be a good idea to record details of items (i)– (iv) in one colour, as they involve A01 content, and items (v)–(vi) in different coloured pen, as they relate to A03 content. An example is given below.

Loftus and Palmer's (1974) study into eye-witness testimony

Aim:

→ To assess how far people's estimates of car speeds could be influenced by misleading information.

Design:

→ The design is independent groups design.

Procedure:

→ 45 students watched seven video clips of car crashes and were asked to estimate the speed of the cars.

→ There were five conditions (of nine participants each) with each condition having a different verb in the question — 'How fast were the cars going when they contacted/hit/bumped/collided/smashed?'

Findings:

Verb	Mean estimate of speed in miles per hour
Contacted	31.8
Hit	34.0
Bumped	38.1
Collided	39.3
Smashed	40.8

Conclusions:

→ Misleading information can affect memory recall.

→ At recall, misleading information is reconstructed with material from the original memory.

Evaluation:

→ Results may be due to demand characteristics.

→ The study lacks ecological validity, as it has little relevance to real-life situations.

→ The study shows causality, because as a laboratory study it was conducted under controlled conditions, showing the effects of an IV on a DV.

Annotated example 3.12

Describe the sampling method used in Milgram's (1963) study of obedience.   (2)

This is an AO1 question, as it requires you to describe your knowledge.

> The sampling method used in Milgram's study was self-selected sampling. Milgram put an advert in a local newspaper asking for volunteers to participate in his study.

The correct sampling method is identified (self-selected sampling), gaining 1 mark. The second available mark is then gained by detailing how this actually occurred in the study.

Annotated example 3.13

Evaluate Baron-Cohen et al.'s (1985) 'Sally–Anne' study.   (4)

This is an AO3 question, as it requires you to evaluate the Sally–Anne study.

> The failure of autistic children to attribute beliefs to others is a deficit specific to them, as the deficit cannot be explained in terms of the general effects of intellectual disability because the more severely intellectually disabled Down's syndrome children performed better than even the normally developed children, as well as the autistic children.
>
> Maybe the results occurred because autistic children do not attribute beliefs to dolls, as they realise dolls are not animate and cannot possess thoughts and beliefs. However, Leslie and Frith (1988) repeated the study using human actors instead of dolls and obtained similar results, which suggests Baron-Cohen's findings are generalisable to real-life scenarios.

Two evaluative points are made here. Both are relevant to the study and both are coherently argued, which illustrates a high level of understanding.

The first point uses the superior results of Down's syndrome children when doing the test to justify the claim of autistic children having a specific cognitive deficit.

The second point, relating to autistic children's results being attributable to their realisation that dolls do not have thoughts and beliefs, is intelligently refuted by reference to a study that suggests this not to be so. (4/4 marks)

You should know

> The importance of writing skills in maximising exam performance.
> How to use your writing skills to answer different types of questions, including selection, short-answer, application, research methods and research studies questions.
> The differences between writing AO1, AO2 and AO3 content for exam answers.
> How to use the PEA strategy in order to write answers with sufficient detail.

4 Writing skills for extended response/ essay-type questions

Learning outcomes

> Understand the different types of extended response/ essay-type questions

> Understand the levels of response marking for extended response/essay-type questions

> Develop good writing practices, including shaping your writing to fully address the demands of the question

> Recognise bad writing practices and understand how to improve on them

> Understand how to construct an effective answer

Types of extended response/essay-type questions

Extended response or essay questions occur in a variety of forms. They will generally require both descriptive (AO1) and evaluative (AO3) content, but sometimes just AO1 or just AO3, depending on the command words in the question. Application (AO2) essay questions can be asked that require descriptive and evaluative content, but have additional marks available for applying elements from a given scenario to support your answer. Essay questions based on research studies can also occur, requiring elements of AO1, AO2 and AO3 content. Table 4.1 gives some examples of different types of extended response/essay-type questions.

✅ **Exam tip**

Your exam papers will contain a mixture of different types of questions. However, you don't have to answer them in the order that they appear. Generally, selection questions, research methods questions and short-answer questions will take less time to answer, so a good strategy is to do those questions first in order to free up extra time to do the essay-type questions which will have more marks.

Table 4.1 Examples of extended response/essay-type questions

Question	Requirements
Discuss ethical issues relating to Milgram's (1963) study of obedience. (8)	AO1 content is required, as relevant ethical issues need to be described. AO3 content is also required, as these issues need to be analysed and evaluated in relation to Milgram's study.
'I think I must be a conformist', said Erika, 'because I tend to agree publicly with members of a group, even if I don't privately agree with them. I like to fit in you see.' 'I think I'm a conformist too', said Nazma, 'but only in situations where I don't know how to behave. I look to others then for guidance on what to do.' Making reference to the scenario above, discuss explanations of conformity. (16)	AO1 content is required, as explanations of conformity need to be described. AO2 content is required, as these explanations need to be applied to the context of the given scenario, and additionally AO3 content is required, as the explanations need to be evaluated in terms of their strengths and weaknesses.
Assess the individual and situational debate in regard to the performance of sports teams. (15)	AO1 content is required, as the individual and situational debates need to be outlined. AO3 content is also required, as the debates need to be evaluated in terms of how they apply to the performance of sports teams.

Different exam boards place different emphases on different types of essay questions and have different mark allocations for them (including the amount of AO1, AO2 and AO3 marks), so make sure you fully familiarise yourself with the kind of essay questions you will face in your exams.

 Exam tip

Although essay-type questions focusing on explanations/theories/models are very common, do not neglect the other possible types of essay questions, for example, those focusing on research studies, approaches/issues/debates, as well as application essays.

Levels of response marking

Essay-type questions are generally marked by reference to levels or bands that describe the qualities required within an answer to gain varying levels of marks. The descriptions for each level vary slightly between the different exam boards, but they tend to use words like 'good', 'reasonable', 'limited' and 'basic' (or they might be numbered 1–4), and the mark scheme for each question will specify a range of marks within each level or band. Depending on its overall quality, the examiner will decide which level your answer meets and will then determine your mark by assessing whether your answer lies at the bottom, in the middle or at the top of that level. Example level/band descriptions are given in Table 4.2, and an example mark scheme is shown in Table 4.3.

Table 4.2 Example level/band descriptions for essay-type questions

Level/band	Quality of response	AO1	AO2	AO3
4	Good	Response shows good relevant knowledge and understanding. Accurate and detailed description.	Response shows good application of psychological knowledge and understanding. Application is mainly evident, accurate and relevant.	Response shows good analysis, interpretation and/or evaluation that is mainly relevant to the demands of the question. Valid conclusions that effectively highlight issues and debates are highly skilled and show good understanding.
3	Reasonable	Response shows reasonable relevant knowledge and understanding. Generally accurate description lacking some detail.	Response shows reasonable application of psychological knowledge and understanding. Application is partially evident, accurate and relevant.	Response shows reasonable analysis, interpretation and/or evaluation that is partially relevant to the demands of the question. Valid conclusions that effectively highlight issues and debates are competent with reasonable understanding.
2	Limited	Response shows limited relevant knowledge and understanding. Limited description lacking in detail.	Response shows limited application of psychological knowledge and understanding. Application is related to the general topic area rather than the specific question.	Response shows limited analysis, interpretation and/or evaluation that is related to the topic area. Some valid conclusions that highlight issues and debates are included.
1	Basic	Response shows basic knowledge and understanding that is only partially relevant. Basic description with no detail.	Response shows basic application of psychological knowledge and understanding. Responses are generalised lacking focus on the question.	Response shows basic analysis, interpretation and/or evaluation that is not related to the question. Basic or no valid conclusions that attempt to highlight issues. No evidence of debates is apparent.

Table 4.3 An example mark scheme for an essay-type question

Level	Marks	Description
4	13–16	**AO1 and AO3:** The outline is accurately described and generally well detailed. The evaluation is done effectively. The answer is clear, coherent and focused on the question. Specialist terminology is used effectively. Minor detail and/or expansion is sometimes lacking. **AO2:** Application is appropriate and links between theory and content are explained.
3	9–12	**AO1 and AO3:** The outline is generally accurate with some detail. There is some effective evaluation. The answer is mostly clear and organised. Lacks a little focus in places. Specialist terminology is mostly used appropriately. **AO2:** Application is appropriate although links to theory are not always explained.
2	5–8	**AO1 and AO3:** The outline is present. Most of the answer is descriptive. Any evaluation is only of limited effectiveness. The answer lacks some clarity, accuracy, focus and organisation. Specialist terminology is sometimes used inappropriately. **AO2:** Application is partial.
1	1–4	**AO1 and AO3:** The outline is limited. The evaluation is limited, poorly focused on the question or absent. The answer as a whole lacks clarity, has many inaccuracies and is poorly organised. Specialist terminology is either absent or inappropriately used. **AO2:** Application is limited.
0	0	**AO1 and AO3:** There is no creditworthy material. **AO2:** Application is absent.

Activity

Download the specimen mark schemes from your exam board's website and familiarise yourself with the mark levels or bands for the extended response/essay-type questions. Use them to mark a classmate's essay to give you some hands-on experience of how they are applied.

Good writing practices to develop

As an A-grade student, it is essential that you perfect the art of 'shaping' your writing, by structuring and organising your answers to ensure the demands of each question are fully met. Various elements of good practice can be utilised to this end.

Command words and mark allocation

As ever, it is important to identify the command words so that you are able to satisfy the demands of the question — remember that essay questions often have two or even three requirements (e.g. describe, evaluate and apply). Using the number of marks available is also important, as it will suggest how long should be spent on each requirement. Make sure you know the mark breakdown for the different elements in essay questions for your exam board, as they may not be stated on the exam paper.

Structure and organisation

Because essay questions are marked using levels of response marking, your answer will be assessed on its overall quality. Therefore, marks are awarded not just for the content in your answer, but also for its coherence, or the way it is structured and organised. This can be achieved by dividing your answer into discrete paragraphs, and having a common thread or 'narrative' that runs through your essay. A-grade students will establish a narrative by linking together different types of evaluative points to form an elaborated commentary. This will demonstrate a high degree of sophistication and depth in your answer. Such elaborated commentaries can include relevant points concerning issues (for example, gender), debates (for example, free will and determinism) and approaches (for example, the psychodynamic approach). You will earn more credit in this way than by making points in isolation.

Signposting and topping and tailing

Another way to gain top marks is to shape your writing by 'signposting' and 'topping and tailing' so that the examiner can see exactly which assessment objectives you are addressing. For example, signpost descriptive points by using phrases like 'One explanation for conformity is…'; and when writing evaluative material, use introductory phrases such as 'Research support comes from…', or 'One practical application of this is…', and then conclude your evaluative points with phrases like 'This suggests that…', or 'This supports the explanation because…'.

Common descriptive (AO1) signposts include:
→ 'One explanation/theory/model is…'
→ 'A second explanation/theory/model is…'
→ 'One therapy is…'
→ 'Another relevant therapy is…'
→ 'One research study is…'
→ 'An additional research study is…'

Common evaluative (AO3) signposts include:
→ 'However…'
→ 'On the other hand…'
→ 'This suggests that…'
→ 'This illustrates/demonstrates that…'
→ 'This implies…'
→ 'A consequence would be…'
→ 'An advantage of this is…'
→ 'An alternative explanation could be…'
→ 'This is supported by…'
→ 'This is challenged by…'
→ 'Not everyone reacts the same way, for example…'
→ 'There may be cultural variations…'
→ 'A practical application is…'

Comparisons

Another effective way of gaining marks when writing essays is to use comparisons. For example, in a question about the social learning theory of aggression, compare the theory with an alternative explanation, such as the evolutionary explanation. Comparisons should be done in such a way as to draw out the strengths and weaknesses of the theory which is the focus of the question, so be careful not to just describe and evaluate an alternative explanation, as this wouldn't be creditworthy.

Exam tip

Practise building evaluative material into elaborated commentaries. Link together several evaluative points on a topic so that they build on each other to produce a sophisticated answer that demonstrates a high level of understanding. Answers that only feature evaluative points in isolation from each other will not gain high marks.

The difference between…

A-grade students will show more evidence of good practices in their answers to extended response/essay-type questions than other students. This will have been achieved by practising such answers over a prolonged period, so that good practices can be developed and reinforced, while examples of bad practice are systematically reduced and eliminated.

Demonstrating depth in your answers

The material you use in your essays should be shaped or written in such a way that it fully addresses the question being asked. The following techniques will help to give your answer greater depth:

→ Use relevant psychological terminology to demonstrate a high level of understanding.

→ Include real-life examples as a form of explanatory detail, to illustrate your understanding of a point being made. However, never use examples as a form of 'evidence' on their own, as generally this won't be creditworthy.

→ Show evidence of multiple sources in your answer and not just material from one textbook.

→ Only use methodological content, such as criticisms of how a study was conducted, if it helps answer the question (i.e. is relevant).

→ Don't be afraid to be a 'maverick' by including unusual material, such as material learned in other subjects (as long as it is relevant), as this will impress the examiner.

Activity

Create lists of specialist terms that go with each topic area you have studied, and practise using them when answering questions.

Summary of good practices

A summary of good practices for answering essay questions is given in Table 4.4.

Table 4.4 Summary of good writing practices for extended response/essay-type questions

Element of good practice	Action
Demonstrate an understanding of the question	Identify the command words before answering the question
Write to the mark allocation	Use the number of marks as an indicator of how much to write
Demonstrate organisation in your answer	Divide your essay into discrete paragraphs
Structure your answer	Have a common theme throughout your essay
Use of elaboration	Build different types of evaluative points into an elaborated commentary to access the higher-level marks
Use of contextualised issues, debates and approaches (IDA)	Include relevant points concerning issues, debates and approaches into elaborated commentaries
Use of signposting	Use phrases that signpost which assessment objectives you are addressing, i.e. AO1, AO2 or AO3
Use of topping and tailing	Use phrases that show where evaluative points begin and end
Use of comparison and contrast	Use comparisons and contrasts with other theories and studies to highlight the strengths and weaknesses of the theory or study being addressed
Use of psychological terminology	Include relevant psychological terminology to illustrate your understanding
Use of relevant examples	Include real-life examples to elaborate your points — but do not use them as evidence by themselves
Use of multiple sources	Use more than one textbook as your source of knowledge
Use of methodological content	Only use methodological content if it answers the question
The maverick quality	Do not be afraid to include unusual content from other sources, e.g. relevant material from another subject

Annotated example 4.1

Discuss biological explanations for schizophrenia. (16)

Show your understanding of the question by identifying the command words before starting your answer.

Structure your answer by having a common theme and sticking to it.

Only use methodological content that is relevant to the question.

Use the number of marks available to calculate how much to write/how long to write for.

Signpost where your descriptive (A01) content is.

One biological explanation is the genetic theory, which sees schizophrenia as inherited through genes passed on to individuals by their families. No single 'schizophrenic gene' is thought to exist, instead several genes may be involved. The more of these an individual has, the more vulnerable they are to developing the disorder.

Research traditionally used twin and adoption studies to assess concordance rates for developing schizophrenia between people with different levels of genetic relatedness. More recently, gene-mapping studies have attempted to identify genetic material shared by sufferers. Several genes have been found that seem to increase vulnerability.

Research support comes from Gottesman and Shields (1966) who performed a twin study to find concordance rates of 75% for MZ twins, but only 24% for DZ twins. As MZ twins share 100% of genes, and DZ twins only 50%, this supports the genetic explanation. This was backed up by Kety and Ingraham's (1992) adoption study that found prevalence rates of schizophrenia were ten times higher among biological than adoptive relatives of schizophrenics. As biological relatives of adoptive children share genes, but not environment with them, and adoptive parents share environment, but not genes, this again suggests a genetic link. Additional support came from Benzel (2007) who used gene-mapping to find variants of the NRG3, NRG1 and ERBB4 genes common among schizophrenics (but not non-sufferers), indicating multiple genes are involved in susceptibility to schizophrenia. However, Avramopoulos (2013) found some high-level schizophrenia families had multiple neuregulin (NRG) signalling gene variants, while others had none. This suggests schizophrenia is not a single disorder, but a group

Signpost where your evaluative (A03) content is.

Link your evaluative points (in this case about genetic theory) to form an elaborated commentary to show a sophisticated depth to your answer.

 Aiming for an A in A-level Psychology

of related disorders, especially as patients without NRG-signalling gene variants had gene variants in a different pathway and experienced different symptoms.

Also, if genes caused schizophrenia on their own, concordance rates would be 100% between MZ twins, which they are not, indicating environmental factors also play a part. Twin studies are also weakened because some studies find concordance rates between MZ twins as low as 11%. Additionally, Sorri (2004) performed a longitudinal adoption study that found that adoptees with a high genetic risk of developing schizophrenia were more likely to do so if they encountered negative parenting styles from their adoptive parents, again suggesting a role for environmental factors. This is backed up by the non-biological family dysfunction theory, which sees maladaptive family relationships and patterns of communication as causative factors. Therefore perhaps the diathesis-stress model, which sees individuals as having varying genetic potential for schizophrenia that combines with the degree of environmental stressors in their lives to form their actual level of vulnerability, is a better explanation.

The dopamine hypothesis sees the development of schizophrenia as linked to abnormal levels of the neurotransmitter. Snyder (1976) believed that an excess of dopamine released during synaptic transmission leads to schizophrenia. Davis (1991) updated the theory, arguing that high levels of dopamine in the mesolimbic dopamine system are associated with positive symptoms, like hallucinations, while high levels in the mesocortical dopamine system are associated with negative symptoms, like psychomotor disturbances.

The neurotransmitter glutamate may play a role too, as there is reduced function of the NMDA glutamate receptor in people with schizophrenia,

Use psychological terminology (concordance rates, environmental factors) in your answer to highlight your level of understanding.

Compare and contrast with other explanations to highlight the strengths and weaknesses of the theory being addressed (genetic theory).

Organise your answer by dividing it into discrete paragraphs.

with dopamine involved, as dopamine receptors limit the release of glutamate. It is possible that genetic factors have a controlling influence over faulty dopaminergic systems (and thus over the influence of glutamate) in schizophrenics, linking together these physiological factors into a more general biological explanation.

Shape material so that it answers the question.

Only select explanations and studies that answer the question.

Research support comes from Iversen (1979) who reported that post-mortems of dead schizophrenics found excess dopamine in their limbic systems, supporting the dopamine hypothesis, though maybe excess dopamine was an effect rather than a cause of schizophrenia. However, Kessler's more sophisticated 2003 study, using PET and MRI scans, found elevated dopamine receptor levels in specific brain areas, which suggests dopamine is involved in the onset of schizophrenia. The glutamate theory links to this as the street drug ketamine induces schizophrenic-like symptoms in non-sufferers by blocking neurotransmission at NMDA-type glutamate receptors, creating abnormal dopamine functioning. This suggests the actions of dopamine and glutamate are linked in the onset of schizophrenia.

Show where your evaluative points start and finish by 'topping and tailing' them.

Use relevant real-life examples to elaborate points (street drug ketamine).

Build contextualised evaluative points concerning issues, debates and approaches into your elaborated commentaries.

A practical application of this is the use of anti-schizophrenic drugs that work by slowing dopamine production to suppress symptoms. However, Healy (2000) thinks drug companies are keen to see the dopamine theory promoted, as it leads to sales that boost their profits. Also, dopamine theory can't explain why sufferers recover slowly when given drugs, as the medication has an instant effect on dopamine levels. Another problem is that dopamine is more associated with positive symptoms. This suggests there are several types of schizophrenia, with dopamine only linking to some of them.

Don't be afraid to use relevant material from other sources to accentuate the breadth of your understanding.

The example essay on the preceding pages shows many elements of good practice. It is organised and structured, sticks to the question throughout and is coherently expressed in an informative manner. Two explanations are fully described (three if the glutamate explanation is seen as a separate theory to the dopamine hypothesis), and the evaluative points are built into an elaborated commentary that includes IDA material showing sophistication in the student's understanding.

Psychological terminology is used accurately, and the methodological content included addresses the question. The content is signposted well as either being descriptive or evaluative, with the evaluative points also being topped and tailed to show where they begin and finish. The material used is well-selected and shaped to fit the question. A relevant real-life example is included, and the non-biological family dysfunction theory is used as a contrast to highlight that environmental factors play a role that biological theories neglect. Additionally, the student is not afraid to make a relevant and unusual point about drug companies maximising their profits.

An essay of this quality is quite commendably drawn from several sources and easily earns full marks.

Bad writing practices to avoid

Just as important as developing good practices in your essay writing is knowing what bad practices to avoid. And failing to develop good practices is the first one!

Activity

Every time you get a marked essay back from your teacher, read the feedback closely and identify one thing that you are doing well and one thing where there is room for improvement — you could use the summaries of good and bad practice to help you do this, or discuss it with your teacher. Then in your next essay, ensure that you repeat the good practice, while also making sure that you address the bad practice. In this way you will consolidate the positive aspects of your written work, while simultaneously improving the quality of your essay writing in incremental stages.

Writing non-creditworthy material

Writing material that won't earn you marks, such as vague introductions and conclusions, wastes valuable time that could have been spent creating creditworthy material. It is the same with writing irrelevant material that doesn't answer the question, such as outlining a psychological therapy when a biological one is called for. Credit will also not be given for including personal opinions that are not justified in psychological terms (such as by the use of research evidence), or for non-research evidence, for example, referring to stories in the media as 'case studies' when they are not. Use the command words to focus your writing, so that you only include relevant material that addresses the question.

Writing generic material

Writing generic answers will not give you access to the higher-level marks — for example, describing and evaluating evolutionary theory in general, when the question calls for a specific aspect of evolutionary theory, such as evolutionary explanations of aggression. Writing pre-prepared, formulaic answers may be an effective strategy for students just looking for a pass mark, but is not worthy of an A-grade student.

As discussed above, writing points concerning issue, debates and approaches is a good way of forming an elaborated commentary, but only if done in a relevant fashion. Writing such material in a generic way that does not directly answer the question will gain little in the way of marks. The same can be said about including irrelevant methodological material. For example, in an essay question about the validity of an explanation, the findings of research studies can legitimately be used to evaluate the explanation. However, commenting on the strengths and weaknesses of the methodology of these studies would not be a relevant means of assessing the validity of the explanation in any deeply meaningful way. It is usually better to spend the time focusing on more relevant material.

> ### ! Common pitfall
> Students often include largely irrelevant methodological content, often of a generic nature. For example, every time an experiment is mentioned some students feel the need to say 'this lacks ecological validity' or 'this shows causality'. Many essay questions concern explanations and theories and your evaluation will be best-served by assessing the validity of such explanations or theories, and not by making low-level methodological comments that give little insight into them.

Writing unbalanced answers

A common bad practice with top-level students is including too much description in your essays. You do not have to write everything you know, but instead you should write enough, and no more, to gain all the available marks. If you over-write your descriptions, you won't have enough time to write your evaluation material and this could easily prevent you from gaining a much-deserved grade A. And remember, if an essay question has AO2 marks for application, you will also have to make reference to a given scenario to gain access to those marks. Make sure you know in advance what the relevant mark allocations are for the different assessment objectives when writing essays for your exam board, as they generally won't be stated on the exam papers.

> ### ! Common pitfall
> Students can spend too long on the descriptive parts of their essay, indeed some students feel the need to describe everything they know about a given topic. More marks are available for evaluation in these types of questions, so it is important to allow sufficient time to write enough evaluative points to get the higher-level marks.

Activity

Find an example of an essay question from your exam board's past and specimen papers and work out what the mark allocations are for the different assessment objectives (AO1, AO2, AO3). Calculate how long you have in the exam to answer the question — your teacher should be able to help you with this. Then work out how long you would need to spend on each element of the answer: description (AO1), evaluation (AO3) and possibly application too (AO2). Have a go at writing the answer, but only spend the requisite amount of time on each element. If you do this on a regular basis, it should become an almost automatic process and will help stop you over-writing the descriptive elements and under-writing the evaluative elements.

Losing focus on the question

A final example of bad practice is wandering away from the focus of the question while writing your essay. This often happens when trying to contrast one specific theory/therapy/study with another. Comparing and contrasting is an effective strategy if it is used to highlight the weaknesses and strengths of the theory/therapy/study being addressed in the question, but it is all too easy to find yourself outlining and evaluating your contrasting theory, and in essence answering a totally different question.

Summary of bad practices

A summary of bad practices for answering essay questions is given in Table 4.5.

Table 4.5 Summary of bad writing practices for extended response/essay-type questions

Element of bad practice	Description
Absence of good practice	Failing to develop good practices in your essay writing
Use of non-creditworthy material	Writing content that does not earn marks, such as non-creditworthy introductions and conclusions
Irrelevant material	Including material that does not answer the question
Use of personal opinions	Including opinions that are not justified in psychological terms
Use of non-research evidence	Including non-psychological 'evidence', such as media stories
Generic content	Providing general descriptions and evaluations, for example, of a theory or an approach
Use of pre-prepared material	Writing pre-prepared, formulaic answers
Irrelevant use of issues, debates and approaches (IDA)	Including points concerning issues, debates and approaches that fail to address the question
Irrelevant use of methodological content	Including methodological points that fail to address the question
Unbalanced answers	Writing too much or too little AO1, AO2 or AO3 material
Losing focus on the question	Failing to address the question throughout the answer

Annotated example 4.2
Discuss the working memory model of memory.   (16)

In this essay I will discuss the working memory model (WMM) of memory by describing its components and explaining how it works. After that I will evaluate it by having a look at some research studies to see if it is correct or not.

Introductions like this are non-creditworthy. It neither describes nor evaluates the model in any way.

The WMM is part of the cognitive approach, which focuses on the mental processes that underpin behaviour, like memory and decision-making. The approach came to the fore in the 1950s and sees the mind as functioning like a computer by converting sensory information into electrical impulses that flow along nerve fibres to the brain, which processes the information to initiate a behavioural response. The approach has a lot of empirical support, and is seen as better than the behavioural approach, as it explains the mental processes that occur between a stimulus and a response and has generated practical applications, such as the development of artificial intelligence (AI).

Generic content (description and evaluation) of the cognitive approach will earn little credit. The WMM is part of the cognitive approach, but the question requires a specific focus on memory, not the approach it is part of.

This paragraph wanders from the question. The answer should be focused on the WMM, not the MSM (unless it is used to highlight the strengths and weaknesses of the WMM).

The WMM came out of the multi-store model (MSM), which sees memory as a system of stores that information flows between, with differences between the stores being those of capacity (how much information can be stored in memory), duration (how long information can be stored in memory) and coding (how information is represented in memory) .The WMM sees memory as controlled by a central executive (CE) which decides which sensory information to pay attention to and then sends information to the appropriate slave systems: the phonological loop (PL) for auditory information and the visuospatial sketchpad (VSS) for visual and spatial information. The PL sub-divides into two sub-components. First is the primary acoustic store (PAS), which holds words and sounds recently heard and is known as the 'inner ear'. Second is the articulatory process (AP), which keeps information recently heard within the PL by sub-vocally repeating it and is known as the 'inner voice'. It can hold about 2 seconds' worth of information and is involved in the production of speech. The visuospatial sketchpad also sub-divides into two sub-components. First is the visual cache (VC), which stores visual information about shape, form and colour, and is known as the 'inner eye'. Second is the inner scribe (IS), which holds information about spatial relationships. All of the slave-system components send information to the CE. The VSS is probably more important than the PL, as I think I, like most people, rely on and spend more time using visual information than auditory information. Another slave component was added later, the episodic buffer (EB); this acts as a general store and can hold information from the PL, the VSS and long-term memory. The WMM was invented by Alan Baddeley of York University. He originally became interested in memory, as he worked on a project for the Post Office to come up with a way of representing people's addresses that they could easily remember using letters and numbers. Eventually this became the postcodes, which we still use to this day.

Trojani and Grossi (1995) performed research into slave systems by conducting a case study of SC who suffered brain damage that affected the functioning of his PL, but not his VSS. This was a case study, so it gives good insight into unusual instances and can help form therapies for such individuals, but as it was only done on one person the results are not representative and cannot be generalised to the whole population. Gathercole and Baddeley (1993) also examined slave systems. They found participants had

An unsubstantiated personal opinion like this is not creditworthy.

The information about Professor Baddeley is correct, but irrelevant to the question, so it won't gain any credit.

The studies in this paragraph have presumably been included to evaluate the model, but they are not evaluated, the findings are merely described. Conclusions would be needed for them to be evaluative, for example saying whether the findings support the model and why.

This methodological content is non-creditworthy. The comments about case studies are accurate, but they do not address the question of describing and evaluating the WMM.

The studies in this paragraph should be signposted as evaluation, for example, by saying 'Research support comes from…'. And as well as being 'topped' (introduced as an evaluative point), they should also be 'tailed' to illustrate the point being made. For example, for Trojani and Grossi, it could be said 'This suggests the PL to be a separate system to the VSS in line with the model.'

Non-research evidence such as television programmes should not be included, as they cannot be considered empirically determined evidence.

problems in tracking a moving point of light while simultaneously describing the angles on a hollow letter 'E'. However, participants who had to track the light and do a simultaneous verbal task had little difficulty in doing so. Alkhalifa (2009) investigated the EB. She reported on a patient with very little LTM ability, but who had a STM that could encompass 25 items, which is more than the VSS and the PL combined. There was also a study done by the BBC on television that showed it is dangerous to talk on a mobile phone while driving a car, as it messes up your working memory and you might crash. The WMM is reductionist, as it does not really consider other explanations. The WMM is also determinist, as it does not see much role for free will.

In this essay I have discussed the WMM of memory, describing its parts, explaining how it sees memory functioning and using research studies to check its validity. Overall, it has some support, but it does have its limitations too.

Too much description is given here and not enough evaluation. Questions like this generally have more marks for evaluation, so more time should be spent on that element.

Including non-contextualised IDA material will attract little credit. It is not explained why the WMM is reductionist or determinist in terms of the WMM.

Conclusions like this are non-creditworthy. It introduces no new descriptive or evaluative material about the model.

The essay in the example above is full of bad practices. It starts with an introduction and finishes with a conclusion that say nothing of merit and waste valuable time in doing so. There then follows some generic material about the cognitive approach, which the WMM is part of: this is accurate but says next to nothing about the WMM, which is what the question is about. The student then tries to compare and contrast the WMM with the MSM, but loses focus and describes the MSM, without using this content to highlight the strengths and limitations of the WMM, which would have been creditworthy.

The next passage, the description of the model in terms of its components, is the best part of the essay. It is accurate and detailed, but there is too much of it, which means the student doesn't have sufficient time later on to write evaluative material for which there probably would be more marks. It also reads very much like a pre-prepared answer that the student has learned off by heart and trotted out in response to the question, but without showing much understanding of the material being used. This wouldn't meet the requirements of the higher-level mark levels/bands.

An unsubstantiated, personal opinion about the VSS being more important than the PL is then included. This is not creditworthy at all and again wastes valuable time. This is followed by some irrelevant anecdotal content about Alan Baddeley, which is true, but has no bearing on the question asked.

The next paragraph is presumably intended as evaluation, but is actually descriptive (A01) content, as all it does is describe the findings of studies without saying what these findings mean in terms of supporting the model or not. The use of signposting, and topping and tailing could easily have made this section creditworthy as evaluative material (A03). Also, the material about the BBC television programme cannot be considered as research evidence and so does not attract any credit. The inclusion of IDA material here about reductionism and determinism is hardly worth scrutiny, as the material is neither explained nor justified as well as not being linked to the validity of the model.

How to construct an effective answer

Some examples of extended response/essay-type questions follow with guidance on how you might construct an effective answer.

Take it further

Collect some examples of extended response, essay-type questions and have a go at creating your own mark scheme. Get a classmate to do the same, then swop your questions. Mark each other's answers using your own mark scheme and provide feedback to each other based on these mark schemes.

Worked example 4.1

Discuss conformity to social roles. (12)

How to construct an effective answer:
- Give a description or outline of conformity to social roles and then provide an evaluation.
- The outline could describe how social roles relate to social norms, the involvement of identification with such roles and how social roles permit understanding and the prediction of social behaviour to bring a sense of order to social interactions.
- The evaluation would probably be centred on how Zimbardo's (1973) prison simulation study informs us about conformity to social roles, though care should be taken to exclude other elements of the study that don't relate to conformity to social roles, such as the aspects of the study that relate more to obedience.
- Evaluative material focusing on methodological criticisms, such as the lack of ecological validity (as the conditions experienced didn't fully represent those of a real prison), would only be relevant if it focused on the validity of the study in informing us about the role of social roles in conformity.
- Remember that the most effective evaluation is created from a number of evaluative points being woven together to form a sophisticated commentary, rather than being a series of unconnected evaluative points.
- A relevant practical application could be that of prison reform. For example, the American juvenile penal system was amended in light of Zimbardo's findings.

Worked example 4.2

Outline and evaluate Piaget's theory of cognitive development. (16)

How to construct an effective answer:
- Outline Piaget's theory of cognitive development and then evaluate it.
- The outline could be constructed by describing how the theory explains cognitive development occurring through the use of mental structures known as functional invariants and variant

structures. The marks awarded would depend upon the accuracy, relevance and clarity of the descriptions and the degree of elaboration (detail), for example, by detailing the processes of adaptation and equilibration and the use of schemas and operations to develop knowledge, as well as outlining the stages of cognitive development, namely the sensorimotor, pre-operational, concrete operational and formal operational stages.

→ The evaluation would probably centre on the degree of research support for the theory. Piaget and Inhelder's (1956) study of a Swiss mountain scene could be used effectively here, as could Bower and Wishart's (1972) study of object permanence and Piaget's (1952) study of conservation of liquid.

→ Additional evaluation could be formed from critical analysis of the model in general terms, such as the neglect within the theory of the important role that emotional and social factors play in cognitive development. Evaluation based on practical applications could focus on implications for the education of children, such as the application of the Piagetian concept of discovery learning.

→ Evaluative material focusing on methodological criticisms, such as Piaget often using research situations that were unfamiliar to children (such as the Swiss mountain scene), would only be relevant if focused on the validity of the theory.

→ Another way of creating effective evaluation would be to compare and contrast Piaget's theory with Vygotsky's theory, in order to highlight the strengths and weaknesses of Piaget's theory.

→ Remember that the most effective evaluation is created from a number of evaluative points being woven together to form a sophisticated commentary, rather than being a series of unconnected evaluative points.

Worked example 4.3

Outline and evaluate studies of conformity.   (16)

How to construct an effective answer:

→ This is a question based around research studies and as such would need to be answered differently to an essay question on explanations/theories/models.

→ The question's rubric demands that at least two studies are covered. If more than two studies are featured, less detail is expected.

→ Outlining of the studies would consist of describing them in terms of their aims, methodology, procedure and findings. The level of accuracy, detail and coherence would determine how many AO1 marks were earned. Popular studies to use would be Asch's (1955) social pressure experiment, which focuses on normative social influence (NSI), and Jenness's (1932) jelly-bean experiment and Sherif's (1935) autokinetic effect study, both of which focus on informational social influence (ISI). A more up-to-date study of ISI could be Mori and Arai's (2010) Asch-type study. You would need to take care not to over-describe the studies — you would just need to write enough content to achieve the AO1 marks available.

→ Evaluation could centre initially on an analysis of the studies in terms of what conclusions and interpretations could be drawn from the findings. The studies could also be evaluated in terms of the strengths and weaknesses of the methodology used (something that generally would not be very creditworthy in essays based on explanations): for example, Asch did not use any female participants, creating generalisation problems, while Jenness did. Ethical considerations could also be highly creditworthy, for example, the fact that Asch deceived his participants and put them under stress.

→ Gender could be a relevant issue to explore: many studies have found that females conform more, for example Jenness (1932), and the reasons for this could be explored (reasons relating to evolution and socialisation would be relevant here).

Worked example 4.4

Colin put an advert in the 'seeking romance' section of his local newspaper. He wrote about how he owns his own home and is managing director of a successful company, as well as about his love of weight training. Katie, also seeking romance, put an advert in the same section, but she stressed her health, beauty, youthfulness and her regular participation in aerobics.

Making reference to the above scenario, discuss the evolutionary explanation for partner preference. (16)

How to construct an effective answer:

→ This is an application essay question that requires AO1, AO2 and AO3 content. Make sure you are familiar with how many marks your exam board would allocate to each of these assessment objectives and only produce enough content to achieve all of these marks. A common mistake with this kind of question is to not apply the scenario to your answer. This immediately limits the amount of marks you could get.

→ A sensible strategy would be to describe the evolutionary explanation first, but making sure that your evolutionary explanation is specific to partner preferences and not just a generic description of evolutionary theory. Evolutionary theory sees natural selection as acting differently on males and females due to the number of gametes (sex cells: sperm and eggs) they produce and how sure they are of maternity/paternity of offspring. The amount of descriptive (AO1) marks earned would depend on how accurate and detailed this part of your answer was. Your level of coherence and your usage of specialist terminology would help convey your level of understanding here and thus help you meet the requirements for the higher levels/bands of marks.

→ Application to the scenario within the descriptive content would also help convey your understanding, as well as being a good way of gaining the available application (AO2) marks. For example, you could detail how Colin is advertising his resource-richness (owns his own home), status (as managing director) and muscularity (love of weight training), while Katie advertises her fertility (health, youthfulness, beauty) and fitness (participation in aerobics). In this way you could explain the attractiveness of male and female qualities that maximise reproductive fitness, but through application to the scenario.

→ For the evaluation, you could provide research evidence that supports and/or refutes the explanation. There are many studies based upon classified adverts, such as Davis (1990) and Pawlowski and Dunbar (1999). The conclusions of such studies should be built into an elaborated commentary which includes other evaluative points, such as the failure of the explanation to address homosexual and child-free-by-choice heterosexual relationships, as well as the preference of some younger males for older females with less reproductive potential.

→ The deterministic nature of the theory could be included as a relevant debate, as long as it is clearly contextualised in terms of partner preferences. A relevant issue could be that of the lack of gender bias in the theory, as it explains male and female differences in partner preferences.

You should know

> **The different kinds of extended response/essay-type question you will face in your exams.**

> **The qualities required in the levels of response mark scheme to gain the higher-level marks.**

> **The good practices of essay writing to develop, including shaping your writing, linking your evaluative points together to form an elaborated commentary, using signposting and topping and tailing.**

> **The bad practices of essay writing to avoid, including writing non-creditworthy, generic or unbalanced answers.**

5 Practical skills

Learning outcomes

> Improve your understanding of research methods
> Develop confidence and motivation when dealing with research methods questions
> Develop an understanding of the relationship between research, knowledge and practical applications
> Gain an understanding of data analysis used in research studies
> Develop practical research skills

Psychology is underpinned by research — it is the foundation upon which the discipline is based. Therefore learning about psychology without undertaking any research is like learning about cooking without ever baking a cake. There is no assessed coursework in A-level psychology, but some specifications require you to conduct your own practical research, and across all specifications a significant proportion of marks are allocated to research methods questions (see pages 44–50), including 10% of the marks for mathematical skills (see Chapter 1). You will receive direct tuition from your teacher on research methods and how to answer research methods questions in an effective manner. One of the best ways to learn about research methods is by conducting your own research. Indeed all the psychology exam boards recommend that students should be conducting regular mini-practicals. By doing so you will come to have a greater understanding of research methods and will perform better on exam questions based on research methods. In this chapter, we will discuss how to plan, conduct and write up mini-practicals.

The role of mini-practicals

Conducting regular mini-practicals will not only improve your knowledge and understanding of research methods, it will help you to develop the practical skills necessary to be a psychologist — essential for those of you hoping to study the subject at university. Hopefully you will be conducting such research studies within your lessons, but if not it won't be too difficult to conduct some mini-practicals of your own in your own time. This would best be achieved by teaming up with one or two classmates.

By performing mini-practicals, you will be developing your knowledge and understanding of:

→ the principles governing the conducting of research (scientific and non-scientific principles)

→ quantitative and qualitative data and their relative strengths and weaknesses

→ how to plan and design relevant studies

→ how to carry out research studies, including the problems that researchers are frequently confronted with, and how to overcome such problems

→ how to generate and collect data

→ how to analyse data by both descriptive and inferential means

→ how to present research in a conventional fashion

→ how to use research as a form of evaluation in examination questions

The difference between...

A-grade students will have regularly participated in the construction and undertaking of mini-practicals, as the depth of knowledge and understanding gained from doing so will be apparent in their exam answers. This will be especially so in their answers relating to research methods and research study questions, and when using research evidence to make evaluative points. Only by developing practical skills through participation in relevant research will it be really possible to develop the skills that allow access to the higher-level bands of marks.

Planning mini-practicals

Planning and carrying out mini-practicals (including data analysis and the writing up of a report) need not take an inordinate amount of time if it is carried out in an organised and structured manner. Indeed, performing your own research can prove to be an effective form of regular revision. You are likely to see the benefits of this in the form of increased marks and higher grades.

You will need somewhere to carry out your mini-practicals. Some of you may have access to a psychology laboratory at your school/college that you can use. Don't worry if you haven't, as any fairly private and quiet room, whether inside or outside of school/college, will suffice.

For some topics, it will be problematic to carry out mini-practicals due to ethical and practical considerations, for example, conducting studies into schizophrenia, cross-cultural differences and longitudinal development (changes over time). So instead, it might be an idea to design suitable studies for such topics and describe how they would be conducted (including statistical analysis) and written up.

It is recommended that you have a research notebook (or a designated section of your subject file) to record the important details of your research. The creation and upkeep of your research notes will form an important learning and revision tool in itself. The best way to achieve this is to have some pre-prepared templates with designated sections for the various categories of information that you will need to record. This should more or less reflect the format in which 'real' research is presented in journals and thus give you an understanding of how this is done and the reasons why it is done in this way. Additionally, you can include some extra sections that explore the strengths and limitations of aspects of research. This will help you to develop your evaluative skills when answering exam questions concerning research methods (and possibly essay questions and research studies questions too).

Templates

Three suggested templates for your research notebook are given below. These are just a guide — don't be afraid to play around with them to suit your needs. Once you are happy with how your templates look, keep master copies, so that you can print off copies for use with your mini-practicals.

1 Research methods template

Figure 5.1 shows a template based on the introduction and aims and hypotheses parts of a research report. It has sections for recording:

→ the research method (e.g. laboratory experiment, correlational study) and design (e.g. repeated measures design), including sections for their advantages and disadvantages to help you develop your evaluative skills

→ previous similar research (as the introduction section of a research report would do)

→ the research aims

→ the hypotheses (if the study is an experiment or correlational study)

Research method and design

Advantages	Disadvantages

Previous related research indicates...

Research aims	Hypotheses
	Experimental
	Null

Figure 5.1 Research methods template

2 Sampling methods template

Figure 5.2 shows a template based on the design/methodology section of a research report. It has sections for recording:

→ the sampling methods (e.g. random selection, opportunity sampling), including sections for their advantages and disadvantages

→ the independent and dependent variables (IV and DV) if doing an experiment — these would be co-variables if performing a correlational study

→ the procedure — probably best done as bullet points

→ any ethical considerations — again probably best done as bullet points

→ the findings of any pilot studies (possibly including any changes made to the procedure, as a result of the pilot study)

Sampling methods

Advantages

Disadvantages

Independent and dependent variables

Procedure

Ethical considerations

Pilot study indicated that...

Figure 5.2 Sampling methods template

Alternatively, you could adapt this template by having the research methods and design section from template 1 here, and just have a section for the abstract on template 1 (a summary of the whole study in terms of aim, design, procedure, findings and conclusions).

3 Results template

Figure 5.3 shows a template based on the results and discussion sections of a research report. It has sections for recording:

→ a results table

→ a relevant graph

→ a verbal results summary

→ evaluative points (probably best done as bullet points)

→ hypothesis acceptance and conclusions

→ future research ideas

Results table	Results graph

Verbal results summary

Evaluation	Hypothesis acceptance and conclusion

Future research ideas

Figure 5.3 Results template

You could also possibly have a fourth template, if you subject your data to inferential statistical analysis, which details:

→ what inferential statistical test was selected, and the reasons why

→ the statistical test formula and calculations (step-by-step)

→ a consideration of the statistical test results in view of the probability level chosen, critical value and type of hypothesis (one- or two-tailed/directional or non-directional), and whether this is significant or not

Conducting mini-practicals

Which mini-practicals you actually choose to do will depend on the topics you are studying. Ideally it would be good practice to carry out at least one mini-practical for each topic.

Try and ensure that you have experience of a wide variety of research methods in your mini-practicals, for example experiments, correlational studies, self-reports. For experiments, again, try to ensure you conduct all types if possible, for example laboratory, field, natural, quasi. Each research method (and type of experiment) presents its own challenges, which are best learned about by direct experience of them.

There now follow two worked examples to demonstrate how you can carry out simple mini-practicals that will be educational and also, hopefully, a lot of fun to do!

Social influence mini-practical

This mini-practical is based on Jenness's (1932) study of conformity, namely informational social influence (ISI). It is a useful study of social influence to conduct, because it is probably the only study of conformity that is not unethical, as it involves no element of deceit.

You can closely replicate Jenness's study by using a large jar full of sweets (it is important to have an amount of sweets that is difficult to estimate, so that it generates informational social influence), or you can use a variation on the theme. For example, you can ask participants to guess the weight of a cake, the number of calories in a cake, or the number of books in your school/college library. Some students have even done it with the volume of water in the school swimming pool, the number of freckles on a boy's arm, and the number of balloons in a car.

For this mini-practical you will need:

→ a jar of sweets or similar (if replicating Jenness's study)

→ some score cards (for individual and group estimates)

→ a data sheet to enter the estimates onto (see Table 5.1 on the next page)

→ standardised instructions (that tell participants what they will be doing and so allow informed consent to be gained, and emphasise the right to withdraw)

→ a consent form (for participants to sign)

→ a laboratory (or quiet, private testing area)

→ two or three researchers

> **! Common pitfall**
>
> A common mistake when conducting research is to use your friends and relations as participants. This should be avoided, as such people are liable to demonstrate demand characteristics — performing in a way they believe you want them to in order to be 'helpful'. It is much better to use participants you don't have social ties to.

Table 5.1 Example data sheet (adapt for the number of participants and groups used)

Participant	First individual estimate	Group estimate	Distance from group estimate	Second individual estimate	Distance from group estimate	Movement of second estimate: closer/ further away/same
1						
2						
3						
4						
5						
6						
7						
8						

Worked example 5.1

Social influence mini-practical

Research method and design

A laboratory experiment (done in a controlled environment) using a repeated measures design (all participants do both conditions of the IV).

Advantages

→ Shows causality (done under controlled conditions)

→ Can be replicated to check finding

Disadvantages

→ Danger of order effects (not possible to counterbalance)

→ Lacking in mundane realism (not an everyday activity)

Previous related research indicates...

Jenness's original (1932) study involved participants estimating the number of jelly beans (an American type of sweet) in a jar either by group discussion or individually before and after group discussion. The number of sweets was difficult to assess (individual estimates varied widely before group discussion), and it was found that the second individual estimates (after group discussion) generally moved closer to the group estimates, and that females conformed more. It was concluded that people seek guidance from others as to how to behave in uncertain situations and that females are more conformist.

Asch's (1935) 'autokinetic effect' experiment found participants' individual estimates of how much a dot of light moved varied greatly, but converged after group discussion, which again suggests people seek guidance from others as to how to behave in uncertain situations.

Research aims

To assess if people seek guidance from others as to how to behave in uncertain situations.

Hypotheses

Experimental (one-tailed/directional) hypothesis: that participants' second individual estimates of the number of sweets in a jar will be closer to a group estimate than their first individual estimates.

Null hypothesis: that participants' second individual estimates of the number of sweets in a jar will not be closer to a group estimate than their first individual estimates.

Sampling methods

→ Self-selected sample of people responding to a poster asking for volunteers

→ 20 participants: 12 males + 8 females, 18–57 years of age, sports club members

Putting up a poster asking for participants to volunteer themselves is a good way to get a self-selected sample. The wording on the poster should not deceive in any way as to the purpose of the study. Details of the sample in terms of numbers, gender, age range and background should be recorded. You would need about 20 participants to make your results representative.

Advantages

→ Sample relatively easy to compile, as it generates itself

→ Volunteers keen to help, so less chance of 'screw-you' phenomenon (where participants deliberately sabotage the study)

Disadvantages

→ Not representative, as volunteers are generally a 'certain type'

→ Increased chance of demand characteristics, as volunteers will be keen to give the 'desired behaviour'

Independent and dependent variables

IV = whether the individual estimate is made before or after a group estimate is formed.

DV = distance of the individual estimates from the group estimate.

Procedure

→ Standardised instructions read to participants and consent forms signed

→ Participants numbered 1 to 20

→ Jar of sweets displayed for 10 seconds

→ Private individual estimates made and collected

→ Groups formed (1–5, 6–10, 11–15, 16–20), group estimates made and collected

→ Jar of sweets displayed for 10 seconds

→ Second individual estimates made and collected

→ Participants thanked and debriefed

You will need to gather together the participants in your laboratory and read them the standardised instructions that clearly and fully tell them the aims and procedure of the study. In this way you can gain their fully informed consent and get them to sign the consent form. The standardised instructions should remind the participants that they are under no obligation to do the study and can leave at any time. In this way you are dealing with the ethical issue of the right to withdraw.

The jar of sweets should be displayed to the participants for a short amount of time (or balloons in a car, or whatever materials you are using), after which you can get the participants to privately record their estimates on the score cards. These are collected in and the data entered onto the data sheet. Then put your participants into groups of about 4 or 5 and get them to discuss their individual estimates and come up with a group estimate. Always use several mini-groups rather than one large group, as this protects against the risk of positive order effects. Collect in the group estimates, making sure they are not communicated to other groups. The jar is presented again briefly and participants again make private, individual estimates that are collected in.

Participants are then thanked and debriefed, by giving them a full outline of what you were doing and what you were expecting to happen. An opportunity for them to ask questions (which should be fully answered) is given.

Ethical considerations

→ *Informed consent* — participants fully informed of the aims and procedure in standardised instructions; consent form signed

→ *Right to withdraw* — emphasised in standardised instructions

→ *Deceit* — none involved

→ *Harm* — no greater stress than in everyday life; participants fully debriefed

→ *Inducement to take part* — none offered

Pilot study indicated that...

→ Standardised instructions were unclear; updated them

→ Researcher spoke too quickly; slowed down speech

→ Jar couldn't be seen by all; jar placed at front

Results table

Movement of estimates	Amount of movement
First estimate closer to group estimate	2
Second estimate closer to group estimate	15
No movement towards group estimate	3

Number of participants = 20

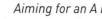

Results graph

No. of participants (y-axis, 0 to 20)

First estimate closer to group estimate: 2
Second estimate closer to group estimate: 15
No movement towards group estimate: 3

Movement of participants' estimates (x-axis)

Amount of movement in participants' estimates before and after forming a group estimate

Verbal summary of results

Two participants' (10%) first individual estimates of sweets in the jar were closer to their group estimate than their second individual estimates. Fifteen participants' (75%) second individual estimates were closer to their group estimate than their first individual estimates. Three participants' (15%) first individual estimates were the same as their second individual estimates.

Hypothesis acceptance and conclusion

The one-tailed/directional experimental hypothesis that participants' second individual estimates of the number of sweets in a jar will be closer to a group estimate than their first individual estimates was accepted.

It was concluded that people do seek guidance from others on how to act in ambiguous and novel situations (ISI).

The one-tailed/directional experimental hypothesis could be accepted on the basis of the descriptive statistics that 75% of participants' second individual estimates of sweets in a jar were closer to their group estimate than their first individual estimates.

The experimental hypothesis could also be accepted (or not) on the basis of an appropriate statistical test, if you wished to carry one out. An appropriate statistical test in this case would be a repeated (related) t-test, on the basis that:
→ a difference (in terms of the DV) between the two conditions of the IV was being sought
→ a repeated measures design was utilised
→ the data was of ratio level

A sign test or a Wilcoxon signed-rank test would also be appropriate, on the basis that if the data is of ratio level, then it is also of at least nominal level and ordinal level. The choice of test, the reasons for its choice, step-by-step calculations, degrees of freedom, critical values and the results of the test could be put into extra sections on your research sheet if you wished.

Evaluation

→ Jenness and Asch's findings were supported

→ ISI may have an evolutionary survival value

→ There are individual differences in conformity levels, as some moved away from a group norm (non-conformists) and some moved neither towards nor away from a group norm (independents)

→ The findings don't explain why people sometimes conform to obviously wrong answers

Future research ideas

→ Test the effect of legitimate authority upon conformity by having researchers dressed in white lab coats as per Milgram's study

→ Assess whether females conform more as per Jenness's findings

→ Have different age groups to test the effect of age on conformity

! Common pitfall

Students often believe they have created a results table for their results section, when in fact what they have created is a data table (which goes in the appendices at the back of the practical write-up). The difference between the two is that a data table contains all the raw unprocessed scores generated from conducting the research, while a results table contains summaries of the data in terms of (where relevant) totals, measures of dispersion and measures of central tendency.

The difference between...

A-grade students will show complete understanding of specific areas of research methods — for example, the role of pilot studies or why the counterbalancing of order effects is important (and how this would be achieved) — attained by regular mini-practicals. Other students with less experience of mini-practicals will not be able to answer questions on these aspects of research methods in a fully effective manner.

Attractiveness mini-practical

This mini-practical is based on Murstein's (1972) matching hypothesis study of relationships, which sees people as seeking to form relationships with partners of similar perceived levels of attractiveness, as this would reduce the chances of them being subsequently rejected in favour of someone more attractive. It differs slightly from Murstein's study as, in this mini-practical, female participants only judge male images and male participants only judge female images so that more honest ratings (especially from males) are given.

You will need to obtain images of couples in relationships — a good source for these is the marriages section of your local newspaper or the internet. Using images from these sources is ethical, because the people in the images have put them into the public domain. It is important that the images are of similar size in order to reduce the chances of confounding variables. Headshots are therefore a good idea. You will need printed pictures of about ten couples. Use scissors to separate the male images from the female images. Stick the female images on to a piece of card and label them A to J, and do the same for the male images (female A should relate to male A and so on).

In addition, you will need:

→ ratings cards for participants to record their ratings on

→ a data sheet to enter the ratings onto (this will record all participants' ratings for all images being assessed, as well as the total scores and mean ratings — see Table 5.2 below)

→ standardised instructions (that tell participants what they will be doing and so allow informed consent to be gained, and emphasise the right to withdraw)

→ consent forms (for participants to sign)

→ a laboratory (or quiet, private testing area)

→ two researchers

Table 5.2 Example data sheet (adapt for the number of female images and number of participants used; a similar data sheet will be required for the male photographs rated by female participants)

Participant number		Ratings for each female photograph									
		A	B	C	D	E	F	G	H	I	J
Males	1										
	2										
	3										
	4										
	5										

Worked example 5.2

Attractiveness mini-practical

Research method and design

A correlational study using two co-variables.

Advantages

→ Allows relationships to be studied in way not possible by experimentation

→ Shows the strength and direction of associations

Disadvantages

→ Not done under controlled conditions, so doesn't show causality

→ Doesn't show the influence of other non-tested variables

Previous related research indicates...

Murstein's (1972) study involved judges rating pictures of people in relationships on their level of attractiveness. People in relationships tended to be of similar perceived levels of attractiveness, so it was concluded that people seek others of similar levels of attractiveness to form relationships with.

Taylor et al. (2011) assessed the matching hypothesis by getting people to rate pictures and profiles from online dating agencies. People tended to contact those more attractive than they were, but replied more to those who had similar levels of perceived attractiveness, supporting the matching hypothesis.

Research aims

To assess if heterosexual people seek romantic relationships with others of similar perceived levels of physical attractiveness.

Hypotheses

Correlational (one-tailed/directional) hypothesis: there will be a positive relationship between the mean physical attractiveness ratings of men and the mean physical attractiveness ratings of women in romantic relationships.

Null hypothesis: there will be no relationship between the mean physical attractiveness ratings of men and the mean physical attractiveness ratings of women in romantic relationships.

Sampling methods

➡ Opportunity sample (those available)

➡ 20 participants: 10 female and 10 male, aged 16–19 years, students at two colleges in the Scottish Highlands

Advantages

➡ Ease of formation — use is made of who is readily available

Disadvantages

➡ Unrepresentative — not all elements of a population may be available

➡ Self-selection —as participants can decline to take part, the sample becomes self-selected

Any sampling method could be used, but an opportunity sample is described here.

Independent and dependent variables

Co-variable 1 = mean estimates of male partner attractiveness rankings.

Co-variable 2 = mean estimates of female partner attractiveness ratings.

Procedure

➡ Standardised instructions read to participants and consent forms signed

➡ Female participants individually rate male images onto rating cards

➡ Male participants individually rate female images onto rating cards

➡ Ratings transferred onto data sheet

➡ Participants thanked and debriefed

You will need to gather together the participants in your laboratory and read them the standardised instructions that clearly and fully tell them the aims and procedure of the study. In this way you can gain their fully informed consent and get them to sign the consent form. The standardised instructions should remind the participants that they are under no obligation to do the study and can leave at any time. In this way you are dealing with the ethical issue of the right to withdraw.

Then, in your laboratory or a quiet, private testing area, get the female participants to individually rate each of the male images from 1 to 10 (where 1 = very physically unattractive and 10 = very physically attractive), entering their ratings on a score card. These ratings will later be transferred to the data sheet. Male participants do the same, but for the female images.

When participants have completed their ratings they should be thanked and debriefed, by giving them a full outline of what you were investigating and what you were expecting to happen. An opportunity for them to ask questions (which should be fully answered) is given.

Ethical considerations

→ *Informed consent* — participants fully informed of the aims and procedure in the standardised instructions; consent forms signed

→ *Right to withdraw* — emphasised in the standardised instructions

→ *Deceit* — none involved

→ *Harm* — no greater stress than in everyday life; participants fully debriefed

→ *Inducement to take part* — none offered

Pilot study indicated that...

→ Standardised instructions read too quickly; were subsequently read more slowly

→ Two female images were very blurry; were reprinted in clearer fashion

Results table

Male partners	Mean attractiveness rating	Ranking	Female partners	Mean attractiveness rating	Ranking
A	7.2	3	A	7.8	4
B	2.0	10	B	4.0	9
C	6.0	5	C	8.0	3
D	5.2	6	D	5.0	7
E	3.0	9	E	3.0	10
F	4.0	8	F	4.5	8
G	6.9	4	G	6.8	5
H	7.5	2	H	8.4	2
I	8.0	1	I	9.0	1
J	5.0	7	J	6.0	6

Ranking key:

1 = highest/most attractive

10 = lowest/least attractive

Results graph

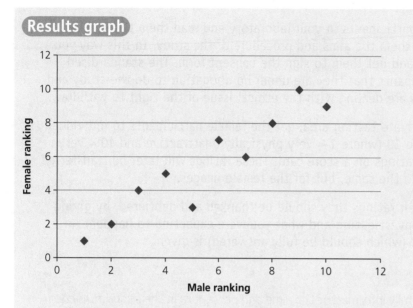

Scattergram showing relationship between male and female romantic partners' perceived physical attractiveness ratings

Verbal summary of results

→ A strong positive correlation between ratings of perceived attractiveness in male and female romantic partners was found.

→ Three couples had identical ranking, six couples were within one ranking point of each other, and one couple was within two ranking points of each other.

→ Seven female partners had a higher perceived mean attractiveness rating than their male partners; two male partners had a higher perceived mean attractiveness rating than their female partners; one couple had identical perceived mean attractiveness ratings.

Hypothesis acceptance and conclusion

The one-tailed/directional correlational hypothesis that there will be a positive relationship between the mean physical attractiveness ratings of men and the mean physical attractiveness ratings of women in romantic relationships is accepted.

It was concluded that:

→ Heterosexual people seek romantic partners of similar perceived physical attractiveness

→ Female partners tend to be slightly more physically attractive than their male partners

The one-tailed/directional correlational hypothesis could be accepted on the basis of the descriptive statistics (that 30% of heterosexual romantic couples had identical perceived physical attractiveness rankings, 60% were within one ranking point of each other and 10% were within two ranking points of each other).

The correlational hypothesis could also be accepted (or not) on the basis of an appropriate statistical test if you wished to carry one out. An appropriate statistical test in this case would be a Spearman's rho test, on the basis that:
→ an association between values of the two co-variables was being sought
→ a correlational design was utilised
→ the data was of at least ratio level

    Aiming for an A in A-level Psychology

A Pearson's Product Moment test would also be appropriate, if the data was assumed to additionally be of ratio level. The choice of test, the reasons for its choice, step-by-step calculations, degrees of freedom, critical values and the results of the test could be put into extra sections on your research sheet if you wished.

Evaluation

→ Maybe people are attracted to others of similar attractiveness due to feelings of insecurity (being rejected for someone more attractive)

→ Evolutionary theory sees physical attractiveness as more important in females (somewhat supported by the findings)

→ The findings support social exchange theory — that people with similar levels of attractiveness are more able to reward each other

→ Static images don't reflect real-life judgements; using video clips would have been better

→ Images were mainly of young people getting married — the findings don't apply to relationships over time

Future research ideas

→ Use images of homosexuals to see if the findings are similar

→ Use images of different-aged people to see if findings are age-specific

Other suggestions for mini-practicals

Which mini-practicals you should attempt will depend on your exam board and the specific topics you are studying. However, it is strongly recommended that you do perform examples of naturalistic observations and self-reports (interviews, questionnaires and surveys) in order to get some direct experience of them to aid your learning. Case studies are more difficult to perform and so should probably be designed rather than actually being carried out. As stated earlier, this will probably also be the best strategy for cross-cultural and longitudinal studies, as well as topics where conducting research would be impractical or unethical.

Suggestion for naturalistic observation: investigate eating behaviour by classifying items available in your school/college canteen as either healthy or unhealthy and then observing if there are differences in male and female healthy eating behaviour. At least two observers would be needed to establish inter-observer reliability.

Suggestion for self-report: investigate definitions of abnormality by designing and administering a questionnaire (or interview) that investigates the degree to which participants meet Jahoda's characteristics for ideal health. The questions asked could be framed so that they generate qualitative, as well as quantitative data. This would give you an opportunity to get some hands-on experience of using content analysis to analyse the qualitative data.

Take it further

A good way to generate some ideas for mini-practicals is to read through the reports of classic psychological studies, most of which can be found on the internet. Then consider how you could perform versions of such studies that explore a slightly different area. For example, Jenness's study of informational social influence could be explored further by seeing if the effect is greater or less (or indeed the same) for older people, or for rural people as compared to those living in urban settings. If you are absolutely stuck for ideas, the research reports often suggest ideas for further research themselves.

Activity

Make a list of all the topics you need to study to cover your exam board's specification. Then try and think of a relevant mini-practical that you could do for each topic. These should be fairly simple to carry out, ethical in nature and not hazardous to you or the participants in any way. It is a good idea to check your ideas with your teacher before you go ahead with them. For topics that by their nature present ethical or practical problems, such as researching mental disorders or carrying out longitudinal studies to assess development, it is a good idea to just design a study, but not actually carry it out.

You should know

> The essential role of practical research skills in psychology.
> The importance of conducting mini-practicals as a learning tool.
> How to plan, carry out and write up mini-practicals in a time-effective way.
> The importance of performing mini-practicals as a means of independent learning.

6 Study skills

Learning outcomes

> Understand the importance of being an independent learner
> Develop a regular revision practice as a continual learning technique
> Develop new techniques of learning and remembering
> Know how to revise for examinations
> Be able to construct an effective revision timetable
> Understand the specific requirements of your examination

We have already covered a multitude of study skills in the previous chapters — the quantitative, reading, writing and practical skills. Here we will look at how you can pull these all together and apply them over the duration of your A-level course. The focus will be on revision techniques — those used as an essential learning tool throughout your course, and those end-of-course techniques that will thoroughly prepare you for your final exam papers.

Independent learning

The A-grade student is one who studies independently. In other words, they are self-motivated and self-organised, and they take responsibility for their own learning. What this means in essence is that they are a full-time student, not one who only works in the classroom under the direct guidance of their teacher (though of course they will seek regular guidance from their teacher).

Independent learning means working at least as hard outside the classroom, though in different ways, as in the classroom. Work performed outside the classroom will mainly entail revision of what you have been learning. This can include many methods already detailed in this book, such as wider reading, different types of reading, conducting mini-practicals, re-organising your notes, producing assessed work and so forth.

Independent learning does not necessarily mean working on your own; indeed it is a good idea to have a study friend, someone as motivated as yourself who can perform revision activities with you on a regular basis.

Revision as a learning tool

Many students perceive revision as something that is done in the period immediately before the exams are taken, with words such as 'cramming' used to describe this process. However, although a

The difference between...

A-grade students are more independent in their learning than other students who generally rely more on being told what to do and when to do it. A-grade students will take responsibility for their learning, by being self-motivated and setting goals for themselves throughout their A-level course. This will also prepare them better for university where independent learning is expected.

period of organised and concentrated revision before the exams will be crucial for performing well, revision is actually an essential learning technique that should be incorporated as a regular part of your studying. The material being learned is processed in ways that deepen your understanding of it and thus assist recall of it in meaningful ways.

Regular revision activities

If you are aiming for top grades, little and often is a more effective revision strategy than leaving everything until the week before the exam. Here are some regular revision activities that can be usefully incorporated into your studying:

→ At the end of each week, revise the material you have been studying in order to deepen your understanding and recall of it.

→ Regularly re-organise your notes (see pages 32–33).

→ Have a go at writing your own exam questions (of all types and covering the A01, A02 and A03 assessment objectives). Swop these with your classmates and have a go at answering each other's questions.

→ Plan, carry out and write up regular mini-practicals. This will deepen your knowledge and understanding of each topic, as well as reinforcing your knowledge and understanding of research methods.

Revision activities to help process learning

The best way to revise is to do something additional with the material, something that aids your processing of it, for example reading through a text and highlighting the salient points. Here are a few more examples.

Using your textbook

In addition to reading and making notes from the relevant section of your textbook (and other psychology books available to you), complete all the exercises within it, such as comprehension-style exercises and any exam-style questions, to further aid your knowledge and understanding of each topic.

Using past papers

Attempt past or specimen exam questions (of all possible types and covering A01, A02 and A03 assessment objectives). These can be found on your exam board's website and your teacher may be able to assist here as well. Ask your teacher to mark your answers and give feedback, or swop your answers with a classmate's and mark each other's work. Turning yourself into an examiner is a highly effective learning technique, giving insight into good and bad practice in someone else's work, and is therefore a form of revision in itself.

Using mind maps

Mind maps are diagrams where information about a topic is organised in visual form, generally with a highlighted central theme and associated content placed around it in a linked fashion. Mind maps help you to recall information in a detailed and accurate manner, but they are also useful for producing synoptic links between elements of different topics. Figure 6.1 shows an example.

> **! Common pitfall**
>
> Too many motivated, hard-working students spend a lot of time diligently performing what they think is useful regular revision of their work. Often it isn't, as all they do is read through their notes, generally in an extended reading style. This won't involve much processing of the information and will do little to aid learning.

> **✓ Exam tip**
>
> At the time of writing, most exam board specifications are new, so there isn't much in the way of past exam papers and mark schemes to have a look at. However, exam papers and mark schemes for the old specifications can be useful, as most specifications incorporate a lot of what was there before. So use your exam board's website to access old papers and mark schemes (your teacher may also have them) to give yourself more opportunities to practise writing answers — although do check these questions would suit the current specification.

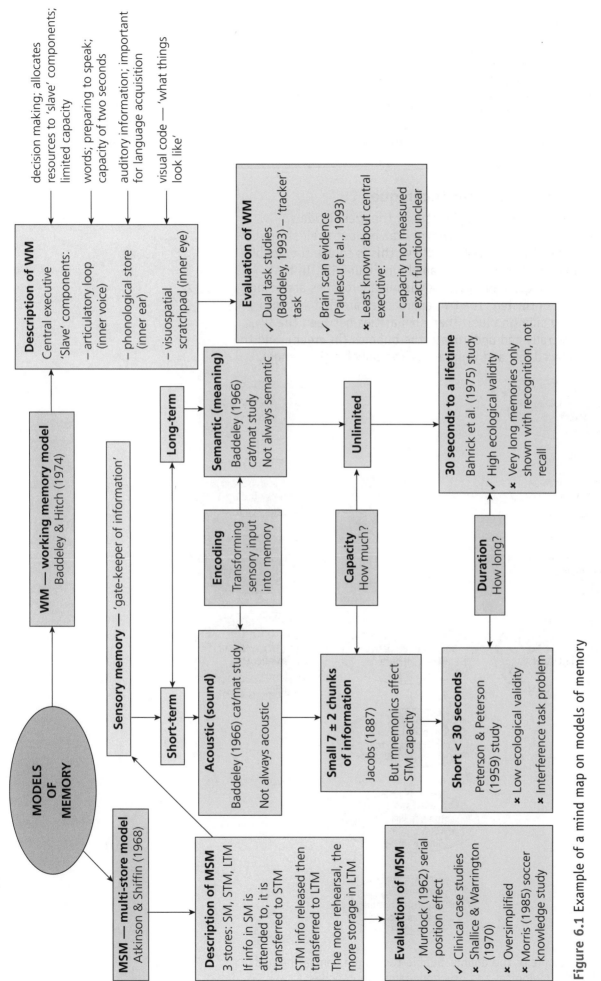

Figure 6.1 Example of a mind map on models of memory

Take it further

Examine the mind map in Figure 6.1 to see how it is constructed and the elements it features, for example, descriptive and evaluative elements. Then, once you have finished studying each topic in your exam board's specification, create a similar mind map for that topic. You will find this a valuable learning exercise that will greatly enhance your knowledge and understanding of each topic.

Using the 'double-bubble' technique

Comparing and contrasting explanations, theories, models, therapies and studies is a good way of drawing out their strengths and weaknesses. A useful way to achieve this is to use the double-bubble technique, shown in the example in Figure 6.2. In that example, the biological and psychodynamic approaches are being compared and contrasted. The two approaches are first put into bubbles side by side (in blue). Then similarities between the two are placed centrally and underneath the bubbles (in green), and the differences placed left and right above the bubbles (in orange).

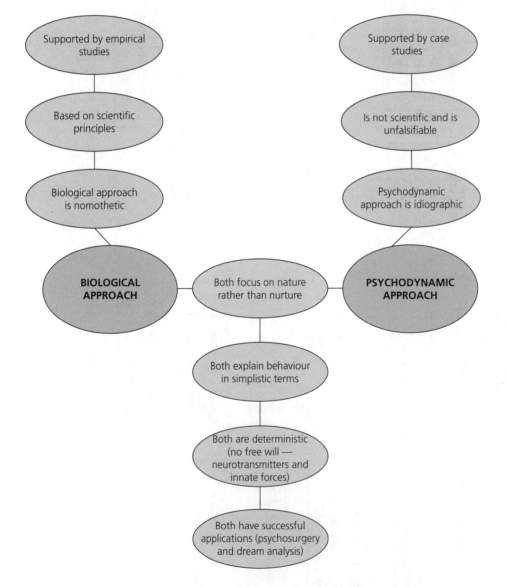

Figure 6.2 Example of the double-bubble technique comparing and contrasting the biological and psychodynamic approaches

Activity

Use the double-bubble technique to compare and contrast, for example the biological and cognitive explanations of schizophrenia. Create two bubbles for the explanations and then add in whatever similarities and differences you can think of. You can do this on your own or in pairs or small groups. Repeat the procedure for another topic you are studying that involves theories or approaches.

Revising for your exams

Although regular revision throughout your course is important, it is also essential to plan and undertake a thorough revision campaign in the immediate period preceding your exams. Indeed many schools and colleges give students a period of time — study leave — in which to do this.

There is no magic formula for successful exam revision, indeed there are many ways to revise and some methods suit some students, but not others. By this stage of your academic career you probably already have an idea of what revision styles suit you, so it may well be a case of adding in new methods to what has worked in the past to meet the extra demands of the A-level questions. However, although you may be tempted to stick with the revision strategies that have served you well, remember that GCSE exams are more knowledge-based than A-level exams, which test your ability to use knowledge in an analytical and evaluative way, and to apply it to given situations.

Leaving revision until the last possible moment is not to be recommended for those aspiring to an A grade. It is stressful to work in that manner and for most will result in not performing to the best of your ability. A much better method is to plan out your final revision campaign in advance, so that it is organised in an achievable manner that will give you confidence and motivation and allow you to ultimately perform to the best of your ability.

What to revise?

You will need to revise *all* topics, especially those you don't like or have struggled with; they could easily feature in the exam questions. It is also unwise to leave out revising something on the basis that it was on the exam paper last year, so will not feature this year, as there is every chance it could be there again. So, when revising for your examinations ensure that you have:

→ a list of all the topics featured in your specification (for the optional topics, you just need the ones pertinent to you)
→ all the necessary materials for revising each topic
→ a realistic exam timetable with all the topics on it, and enough time dedicated to each topic to ensure they are each revised thoroughly

Preparing your revision sessions

When revising, find somewhere you are comfortable revising. For most people this will be well away from others and any possible distractions, but there are no hard and fast rules. For instance, some people work well with background music, while for others it is a distraction.

One distraction to be aware of is suddenly finding 'important' tasks to do. It is quite easy to use up all of a planned revision session by tidying your bedroom, arranging your books in size order and then sharpening 25 different coloured pencils. Remember that a revision session is for revising and nothing else. Make any necessary preparations beforehand and not during the revision sessions. Remember also that you will probably have to revise over weekends and that there will be a lot of distractions to avoid at those times and sacrifices to make. Once you are satisfied with your revision timetable ensure that you stick to it. Some students can revise effectively over prolonged periods, but for most, an hour to 90 minutes a session will be best.

For a topic that you are revising, make sure that you have all the materials you need to hand *before* you start to revise. This includes textbooks, notes, specification details, relevant mini-practical details, past and specimen exam questions (including ones you and your classmates have written), mark schemes and previous written answers (with any feedback from teachers or classmates).

How to revise a topic

Start by reading through the relevant materials (your textbooks and notes) recording the important details. These should be organised into separate AO1, AO2 and AO3 content. You should be able to condense these points down even further onto revision cards (one for each sub-topic, for example the multi-store model of memory). The points recorded on these cards will act as recall prompts (cues that aid recall from memory).

Activity

Have a go at making a revision card. First, use your notes (and other sources, such as textbooks, handouts etc.) to make condensed notes that contain the main points (descriptive, analytic and evaluative) of a topic you have been studying. Then condense these notes down further onto a card in an organised fashion, for example using bullet points and different colours for the descriptive, analytic and evaluative content.

Next, practise answering exam-style questions for this topic — this should be done for all types of questions, for example short-answer questions, application questions, essay questions and so on. At first, you will probably find that you need to have all your learning materials (textbooks, notes, revision cards etc.) in front of you to accomplish this. But when you are comfortable and familiar with this method, advance on and practise answering questions with just your revision cards, and then ultimately without any learning materials in front of you. By doing this you will gradually be creating and familiarising yourself with the actual exam environment. The ultimate test is to answer questions without any learning materials in front of you and to time constraints — there is no use writing over-long answers during revision sessions, as you won't have time to create such answers in the actual exam.

Staying motivated and healthy

If, at the end of each planned revision session, you achieve your goal for that session, for example writing a satisfactory practice answer, then reward yourself in some way. The reward chosen will be different for each of us, but it could take the form of a favourite television programme, a slab of chocolate, a run around the park — whatever pleases you. Such rewards can even be written into your revision timetable, as a form of motivation.

Remember that revising for exams is a concentrated period of study that can last for quite some time, especially if you are sitting exams in several different subjects. Therefore it is important to stay healthy. So eat and drink well in regular fashion and make sure you get an adequate amount of sleep. If you are revising for an inordinate amount of time each day and subsisting on junk food and sugary drinks, you will be doing yourself no favours.

How to make a revision timetable

Draw up a template with the days of the week on, in a way that works best for you as a revision timetable. This might have three slots a day, as in morning, afternoon or evening, or just two half-day slots, or you may prefer instead to revise in hourly slots. The example in Table 6.1 has three slots. When you are happy with your template, print out multiple copies — you will be using one for each week. Then draw up a list of all the topics that need revising. You will need to do this for all the subjects you are being examined in, not just psychology. Indeed, it is probably best to colour code the different subjects: one colour for psychology, another for biology and so on.

Enter the dates of the exams for all your papers in all subjects (colour coded), so you are fully aware of the deadlines you are working to. Put in any non-revision events that cannot be avoided, such as medical appointments or family events, so that you don't create a clash by scheduling a revision session for one of these times. Then enter the topics to be revised — it is probably best to do this in pencil first until you are happy with the arrangement and then enter them in colour. Some students like to have a 'psychology day', while others like to revise different subjects on the same day. Again go for whatever suits you best. What is probably a good idea, though, is to revise the topics for whichever paper comes first, then those for whichever paper comes second and so forth.

Table 6.1 Example of a weekly revision timetable

Day	Morning	Afternoon	Evening
Monday	Psychology: social influence — majority and minority influence	Take Fi-Fi to the poodle parlour	Psychology: social influence — obedience
Tuesday	PE: contemporary issues — gender and racism in sport	PE: contemporary issues — drugs in sport	Biology: grey matter and immunity, infections and forensics
Wednesday	Biology: human musculoskeletal anatomy	Biology: genes and health	Aunty Gladys's 100th birthday party
Thursday	Psychology: models of memory	Psychology: types of LTM and forgetting	Psychology: EWT and improving accuracy of memory
Friday	PE: sports psychology — achievement motivation	PE: sports psychology — goal setting	PE: sports psychology — social facilitation
Saturday	Pigeon racing club meeting	Biology: energy for life	Biology: continuity of life and requirements for life
Sunday	Psychology: definitions of abnormality	Psychology: characteristics of disorders and phobias	Psychology: depression and OCD

Try to ensure there are some spare slots in your timetable in case extra revision of a topic is needed, or because through some unforeseen circumstance you lose a timetable slot (for example, you unexpectedly win the lottery and have to go and be presented with your millions). It might also be a good idea to give a copy of your weekly revision timetable to a parent or similar person. Parents can be troublesome during times of revision, constantly nagging you to revise and so forth. They mean well and feel redundant and helpless that they cannot help you more. So give them a copy of your revision timetable which they can stick up somewhere and see what it is you are doing and when you are doing it. The advantage is that this can also help turn this person into the 'police officer' that you might just need. If your revision timetable says you should at this moment be revising the psychodynamic approach, but you actually are slumped in an armchair marinating yourself in ice-cream, then you might need that reminder of what you should actually be doing.

One of the most stressful and demotivating things about sitting exams is the sheer mass of material that needs to be revised. By constructing a realistic revision timetable you will be able to break down this material into manageable chunks. This will be important in maintaining your confidence and motivational state of mind, as it will allow you the comfort of knowing that everything can be covered in sufficient detail before the examination date rears its ugly head.

Another good way of ensuring your confidence and motivational levels stay high is to periodically remind yourself of why you are doing this — what your target is. If the target is important to you and not one that someone else has imposed on you, your momentum will soon return.

The difference between...

During the exam revision period, while many students will merely read through their notes and textbook in a passive, non-analytical way, A-grade students will do a lot more. They will have made use of a number of activities, including mind maps and revision cards, to process relevant information from a variety of sources to facilitate a deep level of understanding. They will also have constructed a realistic revision timetable, giving them sufficient time to cover all the required topics, and to practise answering exam questions under timed conditions.

Exam skills

Familiarising yourself with the specification

Your exam board website is an incredibly useful resource, and one which is underused by most students. There, you will find your A-level psychology specification which lists all the topics you will have to study and the specific details about what aspects of these topics you can be examined on. Copies are free — download and print off a copy of this important document, place it in the front of your file and get used to reading the relevant sections for whichever topic you are currently studying. It can be used in multiple ways:

→ as a tick-list of what you have to study

→ as a revision check-list

→ as a guide to possible exam questions

! Common pitfall

Too many students beaver away at their studies without ever reading their exam board's specification and so do not develop a solid understanding of just what it is they should be focusing their learning on, nor precisely what type of questions they might encounter in their exams.

It is also a good idea to download and print off past and specimen exam papers. There will be mark schemes for these too, which explain how the marks would be awarded for answers and what kind of answers (including possible content) would be expected to gain a top-level grade. If access to some of the past papers proves difficult (some exam boards don't allow general access to these documents), then your teacher should be able to help you out.

In the exam

Get there reasonably well in advance (and on the right day). Ensure you have everything you might need (and are allowed to have with you) in a small bag, for example, pens, highlighters, pencils, eraser, ruler and so forth. When you are told to begin, do not immediately start writing, but instead engage your brain — read through the questions to ensure that you fully understand them, and are able to make sensible selections between any optional questions. In this way you will be mentally preparing yourself for the task at hand.

✓ Exam tip

There is nothing to stop you writing on your exam paper (though you won't be able to take it away as a souvenir afterwards), so bring a highlighter pen to the exam and illuminate which questions you will be attempting and the command words within these questions. Then decide in which order you will answer the questions.

Whichever board you are studying for, there is no requirement to necessarily answer the questions in the order in which they appear on the exam paper. Indeed, there are all kinds of strategies you can apply as to which order to answer the questions in. This will depend on your individual preferences and the types of questions set by each exam board. There is an argument though for answering the more straightforward, shorter questions first, as they should take less time to answer and theoretically free up more time to spend on the longer-answer questions which are worth more marks.

When you have decided on a question, identify the command words in it, so that you write the 'correct' type of answer (in terms of the AO1, AO2, AO3 assessment objectives). Use the marks in brackets to give you an indication of how much you need to write in order to gain access to all the marks on offer for that question.

It is often a good idea, especially for the longer-answer questions, to jot down a simple plan. This might just consist of a few relevant bullet points that act as retrieval cues and help you in providing some organisation and structure to your answer. Some exam boards even provide designated spaces in their answer books for such plans.

If you finish before the allotted time is up, do not sit there looking smug with your hands folded behind your head; instead, use that time to read through what you have written. You will nearly always find a mistake you can correct, or an answer where you can add a little more detail. You never know, that one extra mark might just make all the difference.

> ✓ **Exam tip**
>
> Answering the shorter and selection-type questions first is a good idea, as if you cannot think of an answer immediately, you may think of one later on in the exam (or some more detail that can be added in).

> ! **Common pitfall**
>
> Many students spend too long writing answers to the shorter types of questions. This wastes valuable time that can be more usefully spent on the longer-answer questions where more marks can be gained, and can have disastrous consequences in terms of the total marks achieved.

You should know

> - The role of independent learning as an effective study skill.
> - How to incorporate regular revision activities into your studying throughout your course.
> - The revision activities that help process learning: using textbooks, past papers, mind maps, the double-bubble technique.
> - What to revise, how to prepare and how to stay healthy and motivated.
> - How to go about revising a topic: condensing your notes, using revision cards, writing under timed conditions.
> - How to make a revision timetable work for you.
> - The importance of familiarising yourself with your A-level psychology specification.

Exam board focus

This appendix looks at what the different exam boards offer in terms of their course content and how they set and assess exam papers for A-level psychology. There are variations between the exam boards, so it is important that you familiarise yourself fully with the particular requirements of your exam board.

This information is relevant for the A-level psychology courses taught from September 2017 onwards. Information about each qualification can be found on the boards' respective websites.

AQA

Core content

The AQA A-level psychology specification is divided into 17 topic areas, 8 of which are compulsory. You will be studying these plus another 3 optional topics, as shown in the table.

Compulsory topics	Optional topics (choose one from each option)
1 Social influence	**Option 1**
2 Memory	**9** Relationships
3 Attachment	**10** Gender
4 Psychopathology	**11** Cognition and development
5 Approaches in psychology	**Option 2**
6 Biopsychology	**12** Schizophrenia
7 Research methods	**13** Eating behaviour
8 Issues and debates in psychology	**14** Stress
	Option 3
	15 Aggression
	16 Forensic psychology
	17 Addiction

Assessment

You will be assessed by three exam papers. Each paper is 2 hours long. There are 96 marks available in each paper, making a total of 288 marks available.

In 2017, the first time this A-level specification was examined, it took 217 marks to gain a grade A* (75.3%) and 193 marks (67%) to gain a grade A.

All three papers must be sat in one summer exam cycle.

Paper 1: Introductory topics in psychology

There are four compulsory sections covering the following topics:

➜ Section A: Social influence
➜ Section B: Memory
➜ Section C: Attachment
➜ Section D: Psychopathology

Each section contains a mixture of multiple choice, short-answer and extended writing questions. 24 marks are available for each section.

Paper 2: Psychology in context

There are three compulsory sections covering the following topics:

→ Section A: Approaches in psychology

→ Section B: Biopsychology

→ Section C: Research methods

Each section contains a mixture of multiple choice, short-answer and extended writing questions. 24 marks are available for Sections A and B, and 48 marks are available for Section C.

Paper 3: Issues and options in psychology

There are four sections covering the following topics:

→ Section A: Issues and debates in psychology (compulsory topic)

→ Section B: Relationships, Gender or Cognition and development (a choice of one topic)

→ Section C: Schizophrenia, Eating behaviour or Stress (a choice of one topic)

→ Section D: Aggression, Forensic psychology or Addiction (a choice of one topic)

Each section contains a mixture of multiple choice, short-answer and extended writing questions. 24 marks are available for each section.

Edexcel

Core content

The Edexcel A-level psychology specification is divided into nine topic areas, six of which are compulsory. You will be studying these plus one other optional topic, as shown in the table.

Compulsory topics	Optional topics (choose one)
1 Social psychology	6 Criminological psychology
2 Cognitive psychology	7 Child psychology
3 Biological psychology	8 Health psychology
4 Learning theories	
5 Clinical psychology	
9 Psychological skills	

Assessment

You will be assessed by three exam papers. Each paper is 2 hours long. There are 90 marks available in each of Papers 1 and 2, and 80 marks in Paper 3, making a total of 260 marks available. All three papers must be sat in one summer exam cycle.

Paper 1: Foundations in psychology

There are five compulsory sections covering the following topics:

→ Section A: Social psychology

→ Section B: Cognitive psychology

→ Section C: Biological psychology

→ Section D: Learning theories

→ Section E: Issues and debates (covering Topics 1–4)

Sections A–D contain a mixture of stimulus and data response, short-answer and extended response questions. 70 marks are available in total for these sections. Section E contains two extended response questions. 20 marks are available for this section.

Paper 2: Applications of psychology

There are two sections covering the following topics:

→ Section A: Clinical psychology (compulsory topic)

→ Section B: Criminological psychology, Child psychology or Health psychology (a choice of one topic)

Each section contains a mixture of stimulus and data response, short-answer and extended response questions. 54 marks are available for Section A. 36 marks are available for Section B.

Paper 3: Psychological skills

There are three compulsory sections covering the following topics:

→ Section A: Methods

→ Section B: Synoptic review of studies (covering Topics 1–5)

→ Section C: Issues and debates (covering Topics 1–5)

Sections A and B contain a mixture of stimulus and data response and short-answer questions. One extended response question is also included in Section B. Section C contains two extended response questions. 24 marks are available each for Sections A and B. 32 marks are available for Section C.

Paper 3 is synoptic by nature (drawing together knowledge, understanding and skills learnt across the different topic areas of the A-level course). The extended response questions in Papers 1 and 2 may also require synoptic content.

OCR

Core content

The OCR A-level psychology specification is divided into three components. All the topics in each component are compulsory, apart from a choice of two optional topics in Component 3, as shown in the table.

Component	Topics
Component 01: Research methods	Research methods: • Research methods and techniques • Planning and conducting research • Data recording, analysis and presentation • Report writing • Practical activities • How science works
Component 02: Psychological themes through core studies	Ten key themes, each represented by a classic and a contemporary core study: • Responses to people in authority • Responses to people in need • Memory • Attention • External influences on children's behaviour • Moral development • Regions of the brain • Brain plasticity • Understanding disorders • Measuring differences
Component 03: Applied psychology	One compulsory topic: Issues in mental health A choice of two topics out of the following options: • Child psychology • Criminal psychology • Environmental psychology • Sports and exercise psychology

Assessment

You will be assessed by three exam papers, one for each component. Each component is 2 hours long. There are 90 marks available in Component 1, and 105 marks available in each of Components 2 and 3, making a total of 300 marks available. All three papers must be sat in one summer exam cycle.

Component 01: Research methods

There are three compulsory sections:

→ Section A: Multiple choice (covering all topics in this component)

→ Section B: Research design and response

→ Section C: Data analysis and interpretation

Section A contains 20 multiple-choice questions. Sections B and C contain a mixture of stimulus and data response, short-answer and extended response questions.

Component 02: Psychological themes through core studies

There are three compulsory sections:

→ Section A: Core studies

→ Section B: Areas, perspectives and debates

→ Section C: Practical applications

In Section A, you will be asked to (i) describe the studies, (ii) compare and contrast the studies, (iii) comment on methodological issues, and (iv) comment on how the studies relate to the key themes.

In Section B, you will be asked about the relationships between psychological areas, perspectives and debates.

In Section C, you will be asked to practically apply your knowledge and understanding of psychology to a novel source provided.

Component 03: Applied psychology

There are two sections:

→ Section A: Issues in mental health (compulsory)
→ Section B: Options (choose two options from Child psychology, Criminal psychology, Environmental psychology or Sports and exercise psychology)

Each section contains short and extended response questions.

Synoptic assessment occurs in Components 01 and 02 (drawing together knowledge, understanding and skills learnt across the different topic areas of the A-level course).

WJEC/Eduqas
Core content

The WJEC/Eduqas A-level psychology specification is divided into three components. All the topics are compulsory in Components 1 and 2, and there are three optional behaviours and five controversies in Component 3, as shown in the table.

Component	Topics
Component 1: Psychology: past to present	Psychological approaches: • Biological approach • Psychodynamic approach • Behaviourist approach • Cognitive approach • Positive approach Contemporary debates: • The mother as primary care-giver of an infant • Using conditioning techniques to control the behaviour of children • Reliability of eye-witness testimony • Relevance of positive psychology in today's society
Component 2: Psychology: investigating behaviour	Principles of research — how psychological investigations are carried out (including social and developmental psychology). Personal investigations — students are expected to carry out two investigations, as specified by the exam board. These differ each year. The details can be recorded in a log book, but this will not be allowed to be taken into the examination. Application of research methods to a novel scenario
Component 03: Psychology: implications in the real world	Applications — a choice of three out of the following options: • Addictive behaviours • Autistic spectrum behaviours • Bullying behaviours • Criminal behaviours • Schizophrenia • Stress Controversies: • Cultural bias • Ethical costs of conducting research

Component	Topics
	• Non-human animals • Scientific status • Sexism

Assessment

You will be assessed by three exam papers, one for each component. Each component is 2 hours and 15 minutes long. There are 100 marks available in each component, making a total of 300 marks available. All three papers must be sat in one summer exam cycle.

Component 1: Psychology: past to present

This paper consists of compulsory questions relating to five psychological approaches, classic pieces of research evidence and a contemporary debate. It contains a mixture of short and extended response questions.

Component 2: Psychology: investigating behaviour

There are three sections:

→ Section A: Principles of research

→ Section B: Personal investigations

→ Section C: Application of research methods to a novel scenario

The questions in Section B refer to the compulsory investigations carried out prior to the exam. This paper contains a mixture of stimulus and data response, short-answer and extended response questions.

Component 03: Psychology: implications in the real world

There are two sections:

→ Section A: Applications (choose three options from Addictive behaviours, Autistic spectrum behaviours, Bullying behaviours, Criminal behaviours, Schizophrenia or Stress)

→ Section B: Controversies (a choice of one from two questions)

Both sections contain extended response questions.

WJEC

Core content

The WJEC A-level psychology specification is divided into four units: two AS units and two A2 units. All the topics are compulsory in Units 1, 2 and 4, and there are three optional behaviours and five controversies in Unit 3, as shown in the table.

Unit	Topics
AS Unit 1: Psychology: past to present	Psychological approaches: • Biological approach • Psychodynamic approach • Behaviourist approach • Cognitive approach • Positive approach

Unit	Topics
AS Unit 2: Psychology: using psychological concepts	Contemporary debates: • the ethics of neuroscience • the mother as primary care-giver of an infant • using conditioning techniques to control the behaviour of children • reliability of eye-witness testimony (including children) • relevance of positive psychology in today's society Principles of research — how psychological investigations are carried out (including social and developmental psychology) Application of research methods to a novel scenario
A2 Unit 3: Psychology: implications in the real world	Applications — a choice of three out of the following options: • Addictive behaviours • Autistic spectrum behaviours • Bullying behaviours • Criminal behaviours • Schizophrenia • Stress Controversies: • Cultural bias • Ethical costs of conducting research • Non-human animals • Scientific status • Sexism
A2 Unit 4: Psychology: applied research methods	Personal investigations — students are expected to carry out two investigations, as specified by the exam board. These differ each year. The details can be recorded in a log book, but this will not be allowed to be taken into the examination. Application of research methods to a novel scenario

Assessment

The A-level qualification is assessed by four exams, one for each unit. This is a unitised assessment, made up of AS and A2. Generally, you will take the exam papers for the two AS units first, after the first year of your AS course, and then take the exams for the two A2 units at the end of your A2 course.

Units 1 and 2 are each 1 hour and 30 minutes long, with 80 marks available each. Unit 3 is 2 hours and 30 minutes long, with 100 marks available. Unit 4 is 1 hour and 30 minutes long, with 60 marks available. The total available marks are 320.

AS Unit 1: Psychology: past to present

This paper consists of compulsory questions relating to five psychological approaches and classic pieces of research evidence. It contains a mixture of short and extended response questions.

AS Unit 2: Psychology: using psychological concepts

There are two sections:

➜ Section A: Contemporary debate

➜ Section B: Principles of research and application of research methods

Section A contains one extended response question linked to the given debates. Section B contains a mixture of stimulus and data response, short-answer and extended response questions.

A2 Unit 3: Psychology: implications in the real world

There are two sections:

→ Section A: The study of behaviours (choose three options from Addictive behaviours, Autistic spectrum behaviours, Bullying behaviours, Criminal behaviours, Schizophrenia or Stress)

→ Section B: Controversies in psychology (a choice of one from two questions)

Both sections contain extended response questions.

A2 Unit 4: Psychology: applied research methods

There are two sections:

→ Section A: Personal investigations

→ Section B: Application of research methods to a novel scenario

The questions in Section A refer to the compulsory investigations carried out prior to the exam. This paper contains a mixture of stimulus and data response, short-answer and extended response questions.